How to Keep Your Kid from Moving Back Home after College

By Bill Pratt, Mark C. Weitzel, Len Rhodes

D1520796

Published by
Viaticus Publishing
4104 Sterling Trace Dr
Winterville NC 28590 U.S.A.

www.ViaticusGroup.com

ISBN: 978-0-9818702-5-0

Printed in U.S.A.

Viaticus Publishing.

How to Keep Your Kid from Moving Back Home after College/ by Bill Pratt, Mark C. Weitzel, Len Rhodes.

ISBN: 978-0-9818702-5-0

This publication is designed to provide accurate and authoritative information with regard to the subject matter covered. It is sold with the understanding that the publisher is not engaged in rendering legal, accounting, or other professional advice. Since individual situations vary, and if expert advice is required, the services of a competent professional should be sought.

This book is available at quantity discounts for bulk purchases.
For information visit www.viaticusgroup.com/books.html

Acknowledgments

To our wives. Without whom we would never have been able to pursue our dreams of financial education.

Contents

Introduction:
Not to Worry

We know this is an exciting time for you and your student. The acceptance letter or letters have arrived and your student has made their decision about how and where they are going to spend the next four years of their lives. New challenges and opportunities await. Yet you are filled with apprehension and concern as you try to help plan and pay for this next big adventure.

College is a lot of things. For your student it is learning new ideas, meeting new friends, having new experiences, and maturing into a young adult. For you it is pride in your student, knowing they will have a bright future, and a sense of accomplishment, for both of you. It is also a scary time for both of you. Your student is worried about assignments, term papers, and group projects. You are likely worried about how best to guide your student through college without being a Helicopter or Velcro parent and how best to pay for everything.

We all know college is a lot of things, yet very few people recognize the huge investment that college is. For both you and your student college is a huge commitment of time, hard work, emotion, and lots of money. Yet most parents and students are not well equipped with the basic personal financial knowledge they need to get the most out of college while at the same time paying as little as possible for it.

This book provides you with the necessary fundamental concepts to help guide your student to the start of a very successful career. By the end you will have a good understanding of what college is all about as a parent. You will know a lot more about all the opportunities college will afford your student and the true and hidden costs of college. More important, you will develop the confidence and skills to advise your student so they come away from college with a great degree, a dream job, and little if any student loans. Best of all, it's a common sense approach that is neither complicated nor terrifying.

What to Expect

You may be feeling a little overwhelmed at the moment and that's okay. Every parent does at some point while their student is in college. This book covers all the topics necessary to help you guide your student through college so they have a wonderful rewarding experience and leave college with the job of their dreams.

This book will not make you an expert in each topic covered. That's okay. You don't need to be an expert. Good decisions in college rarely require a great deal of expertise because they really are not that complicated. They may seem overwhelming at first, but the key is to learn just a few basic concepts and gain a better understanding of the way college works. With this new found knowledge you will help your student gain the insight and skills so that they get the most out of their college experience.

Chapter
The Whole Package:
Why College?

For students whose goal was to go to college, the last two years of high school revolved around getting into a specific college. There are many reasons why you and your student chose a particular college. Perhaps you attended the same college and they wanted to follow in your "legacy." Maybe they followed the school's sports teams for years. Maybe the school is well known for the particular major your student wants. Or maybe the school they wanted was out of reach, so the two of you had to choose another one instead.

These answers only address part of the real question. The question was not, "Why attend this particular college?" The question really is, "Why college in the first place?" Why choose to attend any college?

Is it to obtain a higher education? Or is college simply the next step for them? Did their high school counselor recommend college? Are they attending college because it is what all of their friends are doing? Are they in college to become smarter or to learn new skills? Maybe you gave them a choice right after graduation; either get a job now or go to college.

Your student is attending college for the same reasons everyone else attends college. They are in college to obtain a higher education. Correct? Well, maybe not.

Why Are All These Questions Important?

What if your student had to choose right now between getting a job and going to college? What would you advise them to do? Let's make it interesting. Their only choice is to get a job right now at Mc-Foods Fast Food Restaurant. They will make Mc-Minimum wage and get their Mc-Paycheck each week.

Or they can attend college. For two or four (or even five or six) years they will take exams, cram for finals, pull all-nighters, and write multiple term-papers. In addition, together you will pay thousands of dollars in tuition each semester. It will add up to a lot of money. The average tuition and room and board for a public four-year college is $36,000 over four years.[i] And that doesn't include books, food, transportation, and other living expenses.

What would you tell them to do? College of course!

Now let's make it more interesting. What if you both knew the only job your student could get after college was working at that same Mc-Foods Fast Food Restaurant making the same Mc-Minimum wage and getting their same Mc-Paycheck each week? Now would you advise them to go to college? Of course not! What would be the point of spending tens of thousands of dollars and years of studying, taking exams, and writing papers, just so they could get the same job that they could have if they never attended college in the first place?

Why Are They Really Going to College?

So why really go to college? To get a job. More important, to get a better job than they otherwise could have without a college degree. A college education leads to better jobs and better jobs lead to a better life.

However, before we can begin to really understand how to go from being in college to getting a good job, we have to understand something about the people that do the hiring. It's important to know the employer's perspective. Something most of us never give a thought to is, "Why do organizations buy things?" Let's start with an easier question. Why do you buy things? Look at your house, your car, your shoes, or even your cell phone. Why did you buy any one of those items? You bought them because you liked them. You look good in those shoes and you like driving that car! Your phone keeps you connected to your family and work. You like what you buy.

Organizations do not buy things because they like them or it feels good. Organizations buy things for one reason only: to add value. A fast-food restaurant will not buy a bulldozer because it is not related to their business and the restaurant cannot use the bulldozer to add value to their organization. A construction company will not buy a french-fry machine because it will not add to the value of their organization.

The same concept applies to employees. An organization will not hire anyone and pay them a salary unless that organization believes the employee can add value to their organization. Every employee must add value to the organization or their job will cease to exist. Everyone must bring greater value to their job and to their employer than they cost them if they are to remain employed. Bottom line is that we must add more value to our employer than what we cost them. That is true for your student as well. Your student must bring something to the table that tells the employer "this person will bring more value to the organization than they will cost." That's not real warm and fuzzy, but it is the bottom line truth. Organizations lay people off when they no longer add more value than they cost the employer.

It's All about Value

Of course, the term organization can refer to almost any type of entity. A business or company such as Target or Apple is an organization. A federal or state government agency is an organization. A nonprofit group like the American Red Cross is an organization. A university is an organization. Every organization must add value or it will cease to exist. And every organization will expect each of its employees to add value or that employee's job will cease to exist.

In this sense your student is like any other kind of product an organization buys. An organization will buy your student's time, talent, and energy in order to add value. Your student is a business investment that is expected to provide the organization with greater value than the amount the organization invested in them. They must convince any potential employer that they are the most valuable product available from all of the organization's choices. And employers have lots of choices. Not only is your student a product, but everyone around them is too. They are competing with everyone in their class, in their major, in their college, and everyone else graduating at the same time they do.

If you can get this point across to your student they will begin to understand something that most other students do not. Once they begin to see the big picture, they realize that the real reason they are in college is to get a better job than would otherwise be possible without college. And with that understanding they can begin to do things while they are in college to make sure they are the most valuable applicant an employer can hire.

The Big Picture

Have your student think of himself or herself as a car. Every car has standard equipment such as an engine, tires, and radio. But do they come with leather seats? Do they have the luxury upgrade with built-in GPS? Every employer expects graduates to have the standard equipment to do their job. But is your student the luxury edition that brings a lot of value to their employer? If your student can show a potential employer that they are their most valuable hire, they enhance their chances of getting a good job when they graduate. Not just a good job, but a great job. And not just a great job, but their dream job.

If your student is a car, then their GPA is the engine. Some cars come with more powerful engines than others. Of course, a potential employer wants all of its employees to come with powerful engines or high GPAs, but that's standard equipment. Their GPA is important, but employers also want the luxury edition. In fact, a future employer may accept a less powerful engine in order to get the options they desire. So your student must go beyond good grades and their classrooms if they want their dream job. They must upgrade themselves. It is not going to be good enough to just graduate, even with a high GPA, if they want any chance at all of getting their dream job after graduation.

Your student's diploma will make them marketable, but it will not guarantee them a job when they graduate. A diploma is nothing more than verification from a trusted third-party that they have acquired certain knowledge and mastered certain skills. And that they are now trainable for the job. Employers use the diploma as a prescreening device to tell them your student comes with all the same standard features as that of every other college graduate. It's up to your student to upgrade themselves to the luxury edition while they are in school. They make themselves more attractive and valuable to a potential employer by not only getting good grades, but by acquiring additional skills and experiences beyond the classroom. That's how they begin to get the most out of their college education.

Job versus Career

The big picture for you and your student is that their college education and their degree is a big step to their career, not just their first job after graduation. To get the most out of college it's important to see their education against the backdrop of their career. Their college education is part of their career. They have a very long career ahead of them and their education is the first step in their career plan.

What's the difference between a job and a career? A job is what anyone does right now to earn a paycheck. A career is what is going to be done throughout a lifetime. A career is something that is managed. When your student thinks about their career they must always think, "What is my next step?" What they choose to do today determines what they will be able to do tomorrow. People who fail to properly manage their careers fail to see how actions and decisions taken today translate into future outcomes.

For example, pharmaceutical sales representatives earn a lot of money and are usually hired in their early twenties. For anyone looking to get into a lucrative sales career with many perks, becoming a pharmaceutical representative is a great option. However, in order to get hired, a few years of face-to-face selling experience is mandatory. So if your student wants to get into a pharmaceutical sales career track, they may have to sell cars or cell phones for a few years to gain experience. The point is that they will have to take certain steps today, in this case sell something less glamorous, in order to get to their dream job later.

So what does their college education have to do with their career? Everything your student does right now counts toward how their career will proceed once they graduate. Every class they take, every internship they complete, and every student organization they join has an impact on their future. They should always be thinking, "What is my next step?" What they do today determines their tomorrow. And their education is the beginning of their career.

Attitude

A better understanding of why they are in college is the first step to getting the most out of college. Just as a career is something to manage, college or a "college career" is something to be managed too. It all begins with developing the right attitude.

The right attitude is what makes your student the luxury edition. If they think they can—they can. If they think they can't—they're right. Attitude is more important than aptitude or appearance. It will make or break their career. They cannot control the actions of others, but they can control their response. The most successful people are those with a positive attitude. Employers look for a positive attitude. Your student will earn his or her degree and will learn how to do the work, but it is a positive attitude that will drive their success and advancement from their very first day on the job.

They begin by believing in themselves. Their college already does. Their college had certain standards and criteria, such as a minimum GPA, SAT, or ACT score that your student had to satisfy before they were admitted. The college determined that if your student met its admission standards they can be successful. Their school wants them to be successful. A successful graduate is more likely to make a positive impression in the workforce, lead to more job opportunities for future graduates from their school, and to donate back to his or her alumni fund. Bottom line is that your student's college or university believes in him or her. Your student must believe in himself or herself too.

Your Student is Not Special

While your student is unique, with many talents and positive qualities, they are not special; at least not to a future employer. No one is. This will come as a huge shock to them, and perhaps you too, which may require an adjustment in attitude. Even though they were told all their life by you, their teachers, their troop leaders, and their coaches that they are special – they are not. What about all those trophies that say they are special? Nope, they still are not special. They will graduate along with nearly two million other students. Until your student distinguishes himself or herself, employers will see them as just another applicant for a job position; another resume in the pile. They will not be special. However, they are unique. And they can use that to become special.

Because no one starts out special, it means none of the other two million graduates are special either. Your student can use this to his or her advantage. With no one special, everyone is on a level playing field. And it does not take a lot of effort to stand out from the rest of the crowd.

Most people are happy to be average. And most students are happy to be average students. Average students earn their degree and graduate. Average students find an average job and become an average employee. They lead average lives. And most employers are satisfied with average employees. Almost everyone will be happy with average. Everyone will be happy with average, except your student.

Since almost everyone is satisfied with being average, your student doesn't have to work much harder to stand out from the rest of the crowd. It doesn't take that much more work to be really exceptional. All they have to do is to show up to work five minutes early and stay five minutes late. They should have a smile on their face and a can-do attitude. They should double-check their work and submit it on time. They want to be the first person their boss thinks of when she has an assignment that must be done right and on time. When your student becomes that person they will be the first person their boss thinks of for that next promotion.

Need a New Attitude

So how do they begin to develop this new attitude while they are in college? It's easy. Help them practice being proactive rather than reactive. Get them to ask questions. Tell them if they don't understand something raise their hand and ask a question. They should visit their professors during office hours. If they don't know how something works on their campus, they should go find the answer. They can ask an advisor, the registrar, a financial aid counselor, or any one of the hundreds of people on their campus paid to answer their questions. They cannot wait for answers to come to them. They must go get the answers.

One of the worst excuses in the world is, "Nobody told me." Whose job is it to tell them everything they need to know? It's no one's job; it is your student's responsibility. The list of things that someone is going to tell your student is miniscule compared to the list of things that no one is going to tell them. It's their responsibility to get their own answers.

The next time their professor asks for volunteers in their class, they should be the one to raise their hand and shout that they would like to go first. They can volunteer to be a group leader in a group assignment. They will make mistakes, but that is okay. College is a place to practice and make mistakes so that they don't make the same mistakes once they graduate and begin their job.

The Job Search Begins Now

Nearly 80% of all college graduates move back home with their parents after graduation. That's a sobering statistic for both you and your student. According to the National Association of Colleges and Employers, only 25% of students graduating in 2010 had a job lined up before graduation. Why such startling numbers? After all, these students and their parents spent tens of thousands of dollars to get an education that was supposed to help them qualify for a job related to their career field. Why were so many unable to successfully find employment? The answer is simple. They did not start preparing for their career early enough. They did not create and, more important, execute a plan. Many students think their diploma is a guaranteed give-me-a-job certificate. Nothing could be further from the truth. A diploma is not a job offer. It is simply a piece of paper that certifies they have mastered a skill set, whether it is in biology, economics, management, or nursing, and are ready to go out and learn the job.

Understanding biology is different than understanding how to be a biologist. Understanding accounting is different than understanding how to be an accountant. Employers know this. Most students do not. That is why it is important to go about college in a way that makes them a better employee in their career field. And it is not just about performing well in class.

It doesn't matter if your student is a freshman or a senior, or anywhere in between. Their job search begins now. Seniors should be working with their career office to practice mock interviews, attend resume and cover letter writing workshops, and signing up for interviews. Freshmen and sophomores should also be thinking about their first job after graduation. Students must keep in mind that their education is a means to an end; that end being not just any job, but their dream job.

What does it mean to begin the job search now? It means preparing today for that dream job at graduation, even if today your student is a freshman. At every college, successful graduates return to campus to speak to current students about job opportunities. Recently, on one campus, a successful graduate employed with a national healthcare provider spoke about opportunities with her company. One of the most important characteristics her company is looking for in new graduates is to be bilingual in English and Spanish. Any graduate that has four semesters of Spanish on his or her transcript is much more attractive to this company than graduates with no second language skills. Her company would rather hire a student with a 3.0 GPA and four semesters of Spanish than a student with a 4.0 GPA and little or no foreign language coursework.

If your student is looking for an opportunity similar to what this company is offering, they cannot wait until their last semester to find out that they need four semesters of Spanish. Knowing what a job or company requires early in their college career gives them time to obtain and achieve those skills.

The Job Market

Your student's education is important to their career, but what does that really mean? In 2008 and 2009, the unemployment rate in the United States hit 20-year highs with rates moving above 10% for many states. By 2012 those rates were still in excess of 8%. Many students find the unemployment numbers reported every day by the media quite disheartening. But they really are not that bad, at least not for your student.

When you look at unemployment rates for different education levels you see an encouraging trend (see chart on the next page). From the unemployment rate and the weekly earnings charts you can see that the higher the education level, the lower the unemployment rate. In fact, the unemployment rate of college graduates is much less than that of high school graduates. More important, college graduates earn more money than people without a college degree. That's great news for your student, as long as they earn their degree.

Not everyone gets a college degree. In fact, not everyone even goes to college. According to the National Center for Education Statistics just under 50 percent of high school graduates go to college.[ii] That's right. Less than half of all high school graduates go to college. And of students that go to college only two-thirds will ever graduate with a degree. That means when your student completes his or her two-year or four-year degree they become part of a very elite group of educated individuals. They will have greater employment opportunities and earn bigger paychecks. The key point is that education pays and in more ways than one.

Unemployment Rate

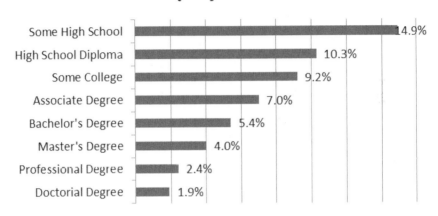

Weekly Earnings

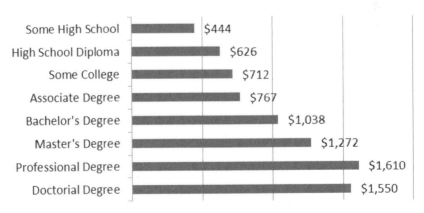

This is all good news. When your student gets his or her degree, it gives them a greater chance of getting a job, keeping a job, and earning a higher salary. That means if they do college right they are more likely to succeed on their own and less likely to have to move back in with you.

Chapter 2
This Side Up:
Planning Properly for College

How can your student get the most out of their college education? It takes planning. Without a plan, they will end up somewhere eventually, but probably not where they wanted to go. Proper planning allows your student to assess where they are, see where they want to go, and see which routes they can take to get there. A good plan lets them evaluate where they are in their college career and identify opportunities that will give them the skills and experiences a potential employer finds attractive. A good college career plan encompasses several key components.

The Three "W"s

The three "W"s are relatively easy questions to ask, but they take time, thought, reflection, and effort to answer. The three "W"s you should ask your student are "What do you want to do?" "Where do you want to do it?" and "Who do you want to do it for?"

What Do They Want To Do?

Your student should begin by asking, "What kind of work do I want to do?" Do they prefer to work inside or outside? Do they want to be a manager? Do they want customer or client interaction? Would they like to work in manufacturing? Would they like to work in education? Do they want to work in the health care industry?

How about for a software company? The choices are endless. It helps to start broad and then narrow it down. For instance, they may be interested in health care. From there they may decide they want to be a doctor, nurse, or physician's assistant. If they want to be a doctor, are they going to be a primary-care physician, surgeon, or some other specialty? The same applies to being a nurse or physician's assistant. Keep narrowing the field down until they have identified their career choice.

"What kind of work do I want to do?" is a very big question. Your student can start answering it by identifying what they like to do. What do they really enjoy? What would they literally pay others to let them do? Is it video games, camping, or playing music? What is it about those things that are so enjoyable? What else is out there that has those same benefits or features? Once they identify the things they like to do, they can begin to investigate what kinds of jobs are in those industries. The best jobs in the world will be the ones that have a lot of things in them that your student likes to do.

Best of all is that they will be very good at a job they like to do. Think about it. They are good at the things they like to do. That's because they practice doing them a lot. Why do they practice doing them a lot? They practice doing them a lot because they like doing them. If they choose a job that incorporates many of the things they like to do, they will be very good at it. They will be successful. Plus they will enjoy their job so much it will feel like they never work a day in their life.

Where Do They Want To Do It?

Once they begin to narrow down what they want to do, it's time to consider where they want to do it. They should begin by identifying one or two, but no more than three, geographic regions that have large concentrations of the kinds of jobs they want to do. Things to consider include whether they want to stay close to family or experience a different culture. Do they want to live on the coast or near the desert? Do they prefer a large metropolitan city or a small town? All are important to their quality of life, but the question of where they want to begin their career must be considered in parallel with their answer to what they want to do.

One thing to consider is mobility. While your student may decide he or she wants to live close to home or in a particular city or region, it is important to understand the correlation between mobility and career advancement. If a particular location is most important, that is okay. But understand that unwillingness to relocate could mean fewer career advancement opportunities within any particular company or within an industry. If career advancement is most important, then mobility or willingness to relocate should also be considered.

Who Do They Want To Do It For?

Now that they have an idea of what kinds of jobs they want and where those jobs are located, they can identify specific organizations or companies where they will apply for a job when they graduate. Since they know these organizations already have jobs they will enjoy and they are located in a place they want to live, they can concentrate on determining which ones will be the best fit for them. Certainly they can research organizations' websites, but they should also visit their offices, speak with managers, and attend their career fairs to get an idea of what they are looking for and what it would be like to work for them.

Prioritize the Answers

To avoid making decisions that seem good for the short-term, but could be damaging or at least not helpful for the long-term, your student should be thinking about the end game. Knowing where he or she wants to be in ten years will allow your student to start with his or her dream job and then walk the steps backwards. What degrees or job experience will your student need to have to get that dream job in ten years? What degrees or experience are necessary to get each of the jobs that lead up to that dream job? Which courses and extracurricular activities does your student need right now to get that first job that will set him or her on that path?

As your student answers the three "W"s, it is important to prioritize them in the order that is the most important for them. Make sure that where they want to live aligns with what they want to do. If it does not, they must decide which is more important. If what they want to do is more important than where they want to do it, then identify places where large concentrations of those jobs exist. If where they want to live is more important, then identify what types of careers and employment opportunities are available in that location. If who they want to work for is most important, then identify where those companies are located and what kinds of jobs are available there. But all three of those questions must also align with where they see themselves in ten years. If not, then your student will either need to adjust the ten-year plan, or adjust his or her answers to the other three questions.

The earlier your student begins to answer the three "W"s, the more they can align their college education in a way to get that first job that will carry them into the kind of career they want. Once they know who they want to work for they can ask people at those organizations, "What do I need to do while I am in college that will make you interested in hiring me when I graduate?" They want to find out as early in their college career as possible what those organizations find attractive in new graduates so they can take the necessary classes, get the appropriate internship, or join the right organizations to demonstrate that they will be the right new employee to meet that company's needs. They want to ask the organization what talents and skills do they need to acquire while in college that will make them the most valuable applicant when they apply for a job. This is a win–win situation. The organization gets a productive new employee, and your student gets his or her dream job.

Your Student the Product

Once your student has an idea of what they want to do, where they want to do it, and who they want to do it for, they can begin to improve themselves, the product. Remember that from the employer's perspective, your student is a product to be purchased so that they can derive value from their talents and skills for the company. Organizations only spend money on products that bring them value. The second part to their college career plan is to put a product improvement process in place so they get the skills and experiences employers find valuable. Your student's product improvement process begins with knowing himself or herself.

Knowing

A big part of your student getting any job is selling himself or herself to prospective employers. For anyone to sell any product, they have to first understand it. Help your student to honestly and critically evaluate themselves. Encourage them to ask, "What are my strengths and weaknesses?" The key is for them to be honest. Everyone has strengths and everyone has weaknesses. Help them to evaluate themselves based on what talents and skills the companies they want to work for will find valuable.

Here's where successfully finding jobs that incorporate many of the things they like to do really pays off. Their objective is to strengthen the talents and skills that an employer values. Since the job they chose has many of the things they like to do, they will be focusing on making many of the things they like to do better. Remember that they are strong or good at something because they practice it. Why do they practice it a lot? They practice it a lot because they like to do it. By choosing a job based on what they like to do they get to focus on those things they like to do while in college.

Your student should start his or her self-evaluation by asking fact-based questions about themselves, such as what is their performance in class, do they have the right work experience, and can they demonstrate communication and leadership skills? Now they should dig a little deeper and look for evidence of specific skills that their potential employer is looking for in new graduates. They want to demonstrate real-life examples of how they have acquired those qualities the employer finds important.

Of course, they will find that they do not possess all the necessary skills and experiences required for their future dream job. They should not panic. It is all part of the process. Help them to remember this is why they are in college in the first place. College is the time to acquire and improve on those qualities.

Improving

Once your student identifies his or her strengths and weaknesses, they should align them with what talents and skills are critical to succeed in their dream job. After identifying what they are still missing to be the most attractive candidate, it's time they begin to acquire those things with their time left in college. Of course, every person is different but there are some common things every employer values. Every organization wants people who are educated, can communicate well, and can lead a team to complete a task.

Completing their degree will bring them one step closer to meeting the minimum requirements for their dream job. Every employer expects your student to come with a powerful engine or GPA. However, the employer also wants the luxury edition. The key is for your student to not just attend class and go through the motions while they are in school, but to take advantage of all the resources and activities available to them.

Do you know one of the most underused resources on a college campus? It is your student's professors. Many students make poor decisions while in college, such as dropping a class too soon or too late, simply because they did not stop by their professor's office to ask for some guidance. Many students who struggle with the concepts taught in the course will use their friends, the tutoring center, and you for assistance. These are all good choices, but the professor should be one of the first places to start. Encourage your student to talk to his or her professors during their office hours if your student needs some guidance or advice with their course work or in their career field.

Part of the self-improvement process for your student is to determine where to spend their time and energy. Your student should ask, "What skills do I need to acquire now based on my answers to the three 'W's?" Here your student will be able to determine which major to choose. Perhaps to get the job they seek, they will first have to earn a graduate degree. Which undergraduate major will help them get into the right graduate program so they can get the job they are seeking? From there your student can determine, with the help of his or her academic advisor, which courses are required for that major. When selecting elective courses, it is a good idea to find out from potential employers which courses they want to see on a transcript, or which skills will be most beneficial in that position or career.

Now, back to the question of, "What skills do I need to acquire now based on my answers to the three 'W's?" An important part of their answer will include two skills that are universally part of any job: communication and leadership.

Communication skills include writing and speaking. Both should continue to improve if they take their assignments seriously and incorporate the feedback from their professors. Their writing skills will also improve by reading books, such as textbooks, popular novels, and nonfiction. Reading comic books, text messages, and celebrity tweets does not count.

Speaking skills improve with the more presentations they give in class, but this may not be enough. Keep in mind their goal is to demonstrate that they are successful at speaking. Their employer will look for practical application of those speaking skills. Here is a prime opportunity for them to stand out from the rest of their graduating class.

Suggest to your student that they volunteer to be first the next time their professor assigns a presentation in class. Suggest that when they have their next group presentation, they ask their group mates if they can "MC" or "host" the presentation. Your student will do most of the talking and call their group mates in to answer specific questions. Your student gets the extra practice and their presentation will stand out from everyone else's.

In addition, they can join organizations specifically dedicated to public speaking such as Toastmasters. The key is for your student to look for opportunities to present to groups, obtain feedback, and practice.

Leadership skills are also very important to every employer in every field. Your student has a great opportunity to gain valuable leadership experience while in college. By starting early with one or more organizations they will have a better chance to get elected to a leadership position. They do not have to run for president; they can be vice president, secretary, or parliamentarian or serve as the chairperson on any number of committees. They can also volunteer for community service projects or work with other students who have similar interests to create their own service project. What is important is that they have a good leadership story to tell a potential employer.

Positioning

All successful products are well positioned. Think of the way chewing gum is advertised and then is right at your fingertips when you checkout at the grocery store. The way for your student to position himself or herself with potential employers is to get the right kind of job experience.

The better the job they want out of college, the better job experience they will need while in college. And not all experience is created equal. A full-time position in their field is the best experience they can gain. It means they understand the industry, and they understand various aspects of the job. Their knowledge and experience helps remove much of the risk that their prospective employer will have to take when hiring them.

However, most experts recommend that a student should not work full-time while attending college full-time. College is your student's number one priority right now. Employers understand this and really value a part-time position within their field while your student is in school. It tells the prospective employer that your student understands some aspects of the field and they are still interested in working in that field. Most likely your student will work at an entry level position while in school and be ready to move up to a position with more responsibility after graduation.

Work experience outside your student's field is also valuable, just not as valuable as work experience inside their field. Having any real-life work experience tells a potential employer that your student at least understands some basics such as taking direction, meeting a schedule, and working with a team.

Internships and Co-operative Education

Another way for your student to gain valuable job experience is to seek an internship or a co-op (cooperative education). Most parents and students are surprised to find out that more than 80% of companies surveyed said they use internships as recruiting tools. In addition, and this is very important, more than three quarters said they preferred graduates with the relevant work experience gained through the internship.

According to the same survey almost half of companies' new graduate hires come from their own internship programs. That means almost one out of every two jobs offered to college graduates goes to someone who interned. So if your student does not intern for the company they want to work for, they may lose out on half of the available job openings. That's how important an internship is for your student to increase his or her chances of finding a job. They should think of an internship as a three or four month job interview.

The best internships and co-ops are paid, are with a company they identified as one they want to work for after they graduate, and allow them to earn course credit. Many, many companies offer internships. These include not just large multinational companies like IBM, Nortel, or Marriott, but local businesses, city, state, and federal government agencies, and many more.

Of course, the easiest time for your student to complete an internship is during the summer when they do not have any classes; however, the competition is stiffer. If your student's major is flexible enough, their best bet is to seek an internship during the spring or fall semester and attend summer school. They must plan well and allow room in their course schedule for both the time and credit hours for the internship. However, the advantage to a spring or fall internship is that most of their classmates will be in school, making more internship opportunities available to them with less competition from their classmates.

Encourage your student to not discount the value of an unpaid internship. They should not let a few hundred dollars keep them from gaining valuable experience that will enhance their resume and may help them secure a job in the future. Unpaid internships should be treated just as seriously as paid internships. They still represent a three or four month interview. The right internship will help them gain great experience, enhance their resume, generate contacts, and in many cases lead to job offers.

Finding the Perfect Internship

So how can your student find an internship or co-op? They should visit the career services office. Unfortunately, most students never even set foot in the career services office on their campus. And those who do tend to do so when they are six-weeks away from graduation. Your student can also consult their specific academic department or advisor for suggestions. Many job sites also have resources online by using the keyword "intern".

Another good approach is to use their connections on and off campus. Encourage your student to talk to his or her instructors, department chairs, and anyone they know who hires in the industry in which your student wants to work. They should talk to anyone who will listen. Your student can use their social network sites, your friends, their friends, and of course you. Most opportunities do not come by chance; they come through connections.

Also, encourage your student to talk to companies face-to-face. They should attend career fairs and ask about internship opportunities. Other opportunities include going directly to individual company websites as well as intern specific websites such as InternJobs.com, InternWeb.com, or GetThatGig.com.

An internship is more than just a checkmark on your student's to-do list like some of their required courses. They want to gain the kind of experiences that will allow them to have smart, complete, and substantive answers to questions during their job interviews after graduation.

Opportunities Are Everywhere

Finally, your student should take advantage of all their opportunities. They can never tell from where a lucrative job offer might come. A professor offered students in her class the choice of doing a term paper or working with a local company on a specific project. Most of the students chose the term paper. Although the term paper was not easy, it was better than having to go off campus to the company's headquarters, meet new people, work in a group, and generally move outside the students' comfort zones.

One student, however, chose to work on a project for a local bank. She had to meet twice a week with a team of analysts, IT specialists, and bank officers. She spent the whole semester developing a cost analysis spreadsheet. It was a lot of work and was all unpaid. Even though she received a good grade for the project, the real payoff came at graduation. She received a great job offer from this bank and is now a vice president in their Information Technology department. Her great job today is all due to her not taking the easy way out. When the opportunity presented itself, she took advantage of the chance to meet new people (especially people who hire new graduates), learn new skills, and impress people with her positive attitude and strong work ethic.

Getting Involved

One of the advantages of going to college is the huge social network. The benefits are fourfold. First is to explore new social interests. This improves social fit and acclimation to college life. Students that isolate themselves from all the campus organizations and activities available to them tend to be less successful at college than those who join a club or regularly stop by the student center. By checking out other social activities on campus, not only do they have an outlet after class, but they also learn more about themselves. This is a great way for your student to begin figuring out the answer to the first of the three "W"s; "What do I want to do?" It is a great way to discover the things they can be passionate about. It also helps your student learn to "play well with others." Since students are so disconnected from others for various reasons, including social media, potential employers would like to see that they are hiring someone who can fit in various social situations. After all, they may soon be sharing an office, a cubicle, or even just a lunch room with others in an organization.

The second benefit of getting involved is meeting new people. In the business world this is called networking. Your student will make new friends, interact with faculty and advisors, and meet others who may currently work in their field of interest. Their interactions with the community as well as faculty and friends on campus will lead to long lasting friendships as well as future job opportunities.

The third benefit of getting involved is it enhances your student's resume. Joining a club or leading some other activity on campus gives your student great stories to tell a recruiter during interview time. Just joining a student group usually results in contributing in some way to a successful community service event. Whether your student helps raise awareness for the plight of two-headed turtles or helps organize a showing of a foreign film, they can now demonstrate useful skills that employers want to hear about.

Better yet, encourage your student to take a leadership position. They will gain all types of experience such as organizing a fundraiser, planning an event, scheduling travel, or attending a conference. Most organizations have some type of budget so your student can reference that on their resume. Any employer will be much more impressed when your student can tell them, "I was responsible for allocating $12,000 annually in activity funds for our organization" rather than, "I have a 3.2 GPA."

The fourth benefit of getting involved is to have fun. Do not underestimate the importance of fun. Fun leads to a positive attitude and a positive attitude could mean the difference between success and failure in college. Your student will never again have so many different opportunities available to them to do so many things than while they are in college. Encourage them to go out and join an organization or activity just to have some fun. Everyone will be surprised by the new things your student will learn.

It does not matter if your student lives on campus, commutes to class, or attends a two-year institution, it is critical that they get involved. If not, they miss out on a large portion of what college has to offer, plus the obvious career benefits. It may be difficult for them to divide their time between class, work, family life, and other activities, but once they find the right balance it will go a long way towards maximizing their college experience. Getting involved is an integral part of your student's college career plan.

Chapter 3
Missing Label:
The Hidden Cost of College

There are obvious costs to college and then some not so obvious costs that most parents and students tend to leave out of their budget. However, there is one huge cost to college that no one really talks about. What is it? The amount of time it takes to graduate.

The Real Hidden Cost

The reality is that the chance of graduating within four years is slim. Most parents and their students end up paying for an extra semester or an additional year or two to obtain a degree. Only about one-third of college students seeking a bachelor's degree will graduate in four years. Slightly more than half graduate in six years.[iii] The average total tuition, room, and board rates at a public four-year college is $15,000 per year, at a private college it is $32,700, and it is $7,700 at a two-year college.[iv]

Delaying graduation by just one year gets very expensive. Most people think it is just the added tuition, board, and other living costs. But each additional year your student spends in college is another year he or she is not working and earning money. Not graduating on time becomes a double edged sword; expenses continue for another year while income is delayed. It is not the extra year's tuition of $9,000 but the lost year's income of 20, 30 or 40 thousand dollars that is expensive.

College is an Investment

College is an investment and it's important that your student keeps in mind why they are in college in the first place. They want to get a better job and to advance their career further and faster than they can without a college degree. College is a pathway to a better life. A college graduate earns about $1 million more than a high school graduate over a lifetime. That is easily enough to repay student loans and all the other money you will spend while your student is in college. The payoff for a graduate degree is even higher. Students who go to graduate school can earn as much as $2 million more than people without a college degree.[v]

Of course a college education is about more than just money. A college degree will make your student more rounded, increase their critical reasoning skills, and give them amazing experiences that they will cherish the rest of their life. There are countless ways that a college degree has value that cannot be measured with numbers.

Yet, it is important to understand that a lot of people invest a lot of money, hard work, time, and emotion into your student's college education. With all this investment being made by you, by your student, and by society, how can you help your student maximize the return on their and your investment?

Maximize Return

If getting a college education is an investment, then the first step to maximizing the return on this investment is to make sure they finish their degree. The second step is to finish as quickly as possible. The third step is for them to choose a major wisely. The fourth step is simply to minimize the costs. It begins by always reminding them why they are in college in the first place. It's to get a better job with a bigger paycheck. Staying focused on the bigger picture will keep your student on the right path. Then you can help them go about it in the most efficient manner possible.

First, finishing college and graduating with a degree is critical. Nothing is worse than shelling out thousands of dollars for a couple of years of college only for your student to apply for jobs with nothing more than a high school diploma. Not only have they likely incurred debt with nothing to show for it, they have also lost several years' worth of earnings as well.

Second, is for your student to earn their degree as quickly as possible for their situation. Although only a third of students who are seeking a bachelor's degree finish in four years, it's relatively easy to do if planned for wisely. This does not mean to speed through by taking the easiest courses or any other ill-advised shortcut. After all, being marketable at the end of the college career is more important than finishing quickly. The point is to be well positioned to receive one or several good job offers upon completion. There are no trophies for winning the race to unemployment. On the other hand, taking five or six years to get an undergraduate degree can mean 25% to 50% more in costs as well as losing out on one to two years of earning a paycheck. Ouch.

If your student has not decided on a major by the time they get to college, and many students have not, they should keep their courses as general as possible their first few semesters so those credits will easily count towards whatever major they end up choosing. For example, when choosing a standard math class, they want to pick the slightly higher level class. The higher the level, the greater the likelihood that more majors will accept it or allow for a substitution.

Third, is to help your student choose a major wisely. Consider how much can be earned with the degree compared to how much it costs or how much will be borrowed to obtain that degree. No one should choose a major based solely on the size of the paycheck. It is critical that they choose something they like to do because no amount of money can make them happy in a job they do not like. However, it's important to understand what the financial consequences are of choosing a major in a lower-paying profession and then plan accordingly. It makes little financial sense to take on $50,000 in student loan debt for a major that leads to a job with an annual salary of $25,000. Are they choosing a major that will afford them a decent place to live, have a car, and manage their student loans?

Minimize Cost

Finally, the goal should be to hold down the costs while your student is in college. The less money paid to earn a degree, the higher the return is on the investment. If they try to live like a professional when they are a student, they will be forced to live like a student when they are a professional. There are several ways to minimize the amount of money needed to earn a degree. For now, let's focus on keeping tuition costs to a minimum.

Community Colleges

Completing the first year or two at a community, junior, or technical college saves money if done the right way. According to finaid.org, the average community college tuition is just 40 percent of the average tuition at a four-year public university. In addition to saving on tuition, your student also saves on room, board, and transportation by staying close to home.

If your student intends to ultimately earn a four-year degree, then spending the first two years at a community college is one of the most cost-effective ways to do so. To make the community college experience cost effective, it is important to map out his or her entire four-year plan. What they take at a community college needs to clearly work in conjunction with the specific degree requirements at their intended four-year college.

If they are already at a four-year school, they can take a summer class or two at the local community college while home on summer break. Why pay thousands of dollars for a course when they can take the same course and receive the same credit for just a few hundred dollars? Plus it keeps them on schedule to graduate in the shortest amount of time possible.

The real key to get the most from any community college is to make sure the credits are transferable to their four-year college. Your student should check with their advisor to make sure the courses they take or plan to take not only transfer to their college or university, but also are applied to their specific major for specific course credit.

College Transfer

One big gotcha is the added expense of transferring between schools and the effect on your student's academic plan. Even though it may make sense to attend a community college for two years and transfer to a four-year school, it can be costly if the transition is not planned for wisely. More often than not, transferring to one or more schools extends the length of time it takes to earn a degree.

If your student is going to transfer to a new school, it should be for the right reasons. It is a bad idea for them to transfer because their classes are too hard, they are homesick, they have a problem roommate, or they do not like the professors. Every college has challenging classes, and almost everyone struggles with homesickness at some point. In addition, every college has demanding professors and problem roommates.

There are many services on campus to help your student with their particular problem. They can check with their advisor for programs that help enhance study skills or they can speak with their resident advisor about a room change to help with a lousy roommate. A visit to the college counseling center may be just the cure if they are struck by homesickness. They can also talk to other students for suggestions on choosing classes and professors. Every college and university offers many different types of assistance. However, it is up to them to find the resources on campus that can help with their problem. Your student's college has a vested interest in their success and they are there to help. But it is the student's responsibility to seek out those services. The school will not come looking for your student and ask how well they are adjusting.

Good reasons for transferring to a new school include finding a better school or major, family obligations, social situations, and of course financial necessity. If your student finds his or her current major is no longer a good fit or they are not being challenged by the course work, these are good reasons to transfer. Also, in the event their current school is no longer affordable, especially if they are paying out-of-state tuition rates, then transferring may be a good option. The important thing is to recognize and plan for the costs associated with the decision to transfer. If the reasons they are transferring are financial, it is important to understand the total cost associated with transferring, including the possibility of losing an entire semester or more of credit hours that the new school may not accept.

Transfer Credit

Many four-year colleges and their academic departments are very particular about the classes they accept from other universities and community colleges. College curricula are not standardized. An introduction to computers class at one school may not transfer in as an introduction to computers class at another school. Transfer credits can be even trickier within specialized majors. In addition, credits may transfer as elective credit only. While the transferred credit hours count toward graduation, they may not fulfill specific requirements for your student's major at the new school.

It is a mistake to assume that transferring will not cause disruptions in your student's academic path. Most transfer students experience some hiccups in their overall academic plan. Before submitting a transfer application, they should have a detailed conversation with an advisor at their current school and discuss options. They should also make an appointment to speak with an admissions counselor at the new school as well as an advisor within the new major to ask if they will receive credit for their course work already completed. Failure to take these simple steps can easily increase their time on campus by another semester or even an entire year.

The same can be said for summer classes taken at another college. There is nothing worse than your student taking a class at a community college only to find the hours will not transfer for like-credit and will only count as elective hours. Always get approval, in writing, ahead of time. Otherwise the transfer credits may be denied or may count as elective hours only.

Not All Schools Are Transfer Friendly

It is critical that a student is academically prepared when transferring from a community college to a four-year school. Community colleges typically have less-rigorous admissions requirements than four-year schools. They also tend to be more general in subject matter. In fact, don't be surprised if your student is asked to provide a syllabus from the community college class so the new school can make sure all the appropriate content was covered before granting credit.

Many new transfer students suddenly find they are low on the financial aid priority list. It is common for the best merit scholarships to go to new incoming freshmen. In addition, many schools accept transfer applications much later than freshman applications. Financial aid tends to be awarded until the funds dry up. Beginning the admissions cycle later than other students makes it more difficult for a transferring student to receive grant aid. If a transfer is in your student's future, encourage them to apply as early as possible and to not submit the enrollment deposit until you and your student know exactly what the financial aid package will be.

Finally, do not underestimate the social cost of transferring to a new school. It is common for transfer students to feel isolated when they arrive at a new college. Unlike the students that began as freshmen, transfer students usually do not start off with a strong group of friends and have not had time to connect with faculty or with student organizations, or develop a social network.

If the isolation leads to depression, poor academic performance, or problems in lining up internships or reference letters, it can lead to both social and financial issues. If your student is transferring to a new school, encourage them to take advantage of every academic and social support service available to acclimate themselves to their new school and to make friends.

Again, if your student is going to take credits anywhere other than the university or college that is going to award his or her degree, make sure credits don't just transfer but will transfer for like-course credit in their major. Not all four-year schools are "transfer friendly." Planning and research are crucial to avoid many of the hidden costs associated with transferring to a new school.

Credit for Nothing

Another way to keep the cost of tuition down is to get course credit for nothing... or next to nothing. Your student should make sure they get credit for any college courses they completed while in high school. If they took Advanced Placement (AP) classes and scored high enough on the corresponding exams, they may be entitled to college credits. They should check with their college registrar or course catalog for requirements. They should also double-check with their advisor that the credit satisfies the degree requirement for their major.

They can also check with their advisor to see if they are eligible to take a CLEP (College Level Examination Program) exam. Each school determines its own acceptable minimum score. Your student receives college credit for very little cost (usually around $100). Plus, they do not have to sit in class for an entire semester to earn those three or four credits.

Also, check to see if the university or college offers any type of credit by exam for their specific major. Typically a student must receive the permission of the dean or chairperson of the department in which the course is offered. They do need to be warned; the grade they receive on the exam usually becomes part of their academic transcript and is included in their grade point average. Once the exam is taken the grade must be recorded and cannot be removed.

College is expensive enough when your student does everything correctly. It is important for your student to not make the mistake of losing a semester or two because he or she did not take full advantage of credits earned in high school or did not properly understand which courses transferred to their new college. Planning correctly for college will mean keeping the tuition costs as low as possible, graduating as timely as possible, and being better positioned to succeed while in college.

Chapter 4
Temporary Storage:
Living On or Off Campus?

What are all the costs of college? Is it just tuition, fees, books, room, and board? Is it the factors used in determining scholarships or financial aid awards? It is all these things and so much more. For now, let's look at the obvious costs of college. Then we'll look at the not so obvious costs and the ones that you and your student have the most control over.

Tuition, Room, and Board

Tuition and fees are often the first costs considered, and rightly so. Unfortunately, all too often they are the only costs ever considered. However, there are many expenses to college that do not show up on tuition statements, but are still necessary in many instances. For example, the privilege of parking on many college campuses can cost hundreds of dollars each year. Textbooks are excessively expensive. It is common to spend $150 or more on a single textbook and more than $200 per class on required materials. Many students often spend $600 to $800 on books each semester. In addition, many classes require specialty supplies, such as calculators, art supplies, portfolio cases, and special software, on top of book bags, notebooks, pens, paper, and the like.

Housing is also an obvious expense, yet many parents and their student never account for all the real expenses of their student living on their own. Total housing costs go far beyond the residence hall fees charged each semester or the monthly rent check written to the landlord. Even living in the residence hall may still require a small refrigerator and microwave, linens for the bed, and a lamp for the desk. Living off campus means a bed, furniture for the living room, perhaps a small dining room set, and pots and pans for the kitchen. Not only do many families forget about most move-in expenses, but often they underestimate those expenses they do remember. In addition, most students tend to underestimate recurring monthly expenses for living off-campus such as Internet, cable, electricity, and many other monthly expenses.

There are many costs associated with attending college, but let's start with one of the biggest money decisions. Will your student live on-campus or off? What are your options and what are the costs associated with this decision?

There are four choices when it comes to housing in college: commuting, living on-campus, living off-campus, and purchasing a place to live. Of course, not all of these options will be available to everyone, but let's take a look at the advantages and disadvantages of each.

Commuting

Of all the housing options available commuting is usually the least expensive. If your student is attending college within a reasonable distance from home, he or she may consider commuting from home. If the college is not close to home, commuting is still possible if your student's aunt, uncle, or other family member lives near the college.

However, commuting is not without costs. The most obvious is transportation. With high fuel prices you must account for the amount of money spent not just on gas, but other transportation costs such as a parking pass, wear and tear on the car, and maintenance expenses. Since your student will not have moved out of the house, you will forgo any savings you would have had on lower utility and food expenses.

If your student will live with a relative near campus, you may want to offer them a small amount of rent as fair compensation. Your student will increase your relative's food and utility bills at the very least. In addition, your relative may be sacrificing some freedom and convenience simply by having another person in their home. Other things to consider are what types of rules and expectations the relative will have such as checking in at night, how late your student can arrive home, and other restrictions on your student's activities.

From your student's perspective the other cost of being a commuter is social. It will be more difficult for your student to get involved in many of the activities and organizations if he or she commutes a considerable distance to campus. Study groups and other organizations tend to meet in the evenings. If your student has to drive home and then return to campus it may be become prohibitively expensive in fuel costs. They may find themselves tired after a long day of classes and unable to drive back and forth while trying to maintain a social life. Remaining on campus all day long without having a place that is close to call home may also make them feel stranded.

Overall, commuting is the least expensive option and certainly makes sense while attending a local community college.

Living On-Campus

Many four-year colleges now require freshmen to live on campus unless they live within a certain commuting area. If this is the case then the decision is already made for your student for their first year. Otherwise, you and your student have a choice.

The social advantage to living on-campus is that your student gets to experience many planned activities for their particular residence hall. They have the opportunity to make friends very quickly and become part of a community. In some instances, such as for honors programs and other specialty programs, students stay in a particular residence hall along with their peers that are part of the same program. While some of these benefits can be had in off-campus housing, many of the opportunities to really establish a core group of friends are best developed by living on-campus

Another advantage to on-campus housing is security. Most dorms have at least one person in charge or on call at all times. In addition, there are fewer break-ins and many larger campuses have their own police force. Most dorms are also commercial buildings built very securely to withstand storms, hurricanes, tornados, and earthquakes.

Finally, students living on campus are closer to campus resources. The library, the fitness center, the student center, and the student theater are usually within walking distance. Just the close proximity of these resources makes it easier for your student to use, meet new friends, and join student groups.

The primary disadvantages to living on-campus are expense and the lack of living space. Of course on-campus living costs are college and location dependent, but in many cases it is less expensive to live off-campus rather than on-campus. This is particularly true if your student's college requires the purchase of a meal plan.

Typically, meal plans are very pricey per meal once you consider the number of meals your student will receive per week. Compare these costs with the cost of having your student do his or her own grocery shopping while living off-campus to make the comparison. Of course, meal plans mean that your student will always have a hot meal available, as most students are not permitted to cook in their dorm rooms.

Keep in mind that your student will still want to hang out with friends who live off-campus. This means they occasionally still purchase meals, snacks, sports drinks, and so forth off-campus. Thus, the expensive meal plan is not entirely comprehensive based on most students' spending habits.

In addition to its surprising cost, residence halls and dormitory rooms are usually small and lack privacy. Combine this with the required roommate and your student may not feel comfortable staying in his or her room very much. This may mean spending more time in the common areas, student center, or library. If your student will spend the time studying, attending class, and joining and leading organizations, then there is no problem. However, when this time is spent socializing and partying it usually results in disaster.

Living on-campus can be a good first step towards independence for your student. He or she will not have to go straight into living on his or her own, planning and cooking meals, and taking care of monthly expenses. You and your student must decide how much independence makes the most sense and what premium you're willing to pay.

Living Off-Campus

Living off-campus is typically as close to independence from parents as most students get while in college. Your student will be responsible for paying rent, utilities, cable, and other household bills. He or she will likely have a roommate and must manage that relationship as well. Many students prefer living off-campus because they get the additional space and amenities of a real home over a dorm room. In addition, you usually save money by not buying the meal plan and splitting most other costs with one or more roommates.

While off-campus housing may be a less expensive option, not all costs will be shared. Each person is usually responsible for his or her own food and other personal items. Distance to campus is also an important factor to consider. It is wise to choose a place that is not so far from campus that your student feels like a commuter student. Living too far from campus could result in more money spent on gas, more money on car repairs and maintenance, and the need to purchase a parking pass each semester. In addition, some students who live off-campus could isolate themselves from campus activities and resources, especially those who live too far away.

When deciding on a place to stay, one thing to include in total cost is whether the unit is on a bus route. If one rental is a little bit more expensive but your student can ride the bus to school it may cost less to live there overall. In fact, maybe your student can eliminate the need for a car entirely.

In many of the larger college communities there are standard student rentals as well as luxury student rentals. Luxury rentals come with many different amenities including a large swimming pool, a game room, a fitness center, free tanning, and other conveniences. You and your student must decide if living in more luxurious student housing is worth the additional costs, especially when many of those same amenities are already available on campus. You are already paying, in the form of student activity fees, for your student to use the recreation center, gym, theater, and other amenities on campus.

Finally, be wary of incentives. Some rental units offer the first-month rent free or a gift card for a certain amount if the student signs a lease within a day or two after looking at the apartment. One free month is great, but if the cost is over $100 per month more than other apartments, your student will still pay more for a 12-month lease. Making a decision too quickly could lead to a mistake, especially if you and your student did not take the time to look at other options.

The Lease

Once your student settles on a place, it's time to go over the lease. It will be a long, complex, and boring document, but it is extremely important that you and your student read it all the way through. A lease is a legally binding contract. Once your student signs a lease he or she is agreeing to all its terms and can be held accountable for everything written in the document. There should be no open blanks on the lease. If something does not apply, such as a pet deposit, they should fill in the space with "N/A," or "not applicable." Otherwise it leaves open the potential of filling it in after the fact to hold your student responsible for something for which he or she did not agree. Of course your student could always produce his or her copy of the lease showing the line was blank, but the strongest defense is to not leave it blank in the first place.

Make sure all relevant information is clearly represented on the lease, such as costs, dates, and penalties. You or your student should talk to a lawyer about any aspects of the lease that are unclear. True, an attorney may charge $100 or $200 to review a lease but that's cheap insurance for the peace of mind knowing that your student avoided costly misunderstandings and big headaches later.

It is critical that the details of the lease be in writing. Legally, the landlord has the upper hand based on what is written on the lease, even if your student verbally agreed to conditions such as no penalty if his or her payment was a couple of days late.

At a minimum, every lease should include the following details:

- Description and address of the property
- Name and address of the landlord or the property management company
- Name of tenant or tenants
- Effective date and length of the lease
- Dollar amount of the rent
- Date and time the rent is due
- Late penalties
- Location where rent is due
- List of all appliances and utilities included in the lease
- List of all services included in the lease
- All restrictions on the property (number of parking spaces, pets, guests, etc.)

When looking at various rental units, understand what it means to look at a one-bedroom or two-bedroom rental. In some cities, a house can be converted into multiple single-bedroom units as long as each bedroom has its own entrance. There is nothing like renting a single bedroom unit only to discover it is a five bedroom house, with a few extra doors to the outside.

It is important to read the fine print and be very careful not to agree to something that is financially damaging or that restricts your student's ability to switch apartments in the future. Avoid leases that automatically roll over to a second 12-month term rather than a month-to-month term. In addition, fully understand which utilities are included with the lease and watch for caps. It is common for landlords to place maximum use levels on electricity and gas that do not come close to your student's actual use. This can be especially problematic if your student has roommates that do not fully appreciate the added cost of going over the maximums.

Finally, your student should be sure all roommates understand their responsibilities. Many first-time renters assume they are only responsible for their portion of the rent. Most leases include the provision that any one person on the lease is responsible for every one of the signers. If a roommate moves out, drops out of school, loses his or her financial aid and has no money, or simply decides to stop paying his or her part of the rent, the landlord has every right to demand that part of the rent from your student. In many instances utilities work the same way. If the utility bill is in just your or your student's name, not only is he or she responsible for the full bill but they will have little or no recourse against their roommates. It is important that your student and all of his or her roommates understand their rights and responsibilities before they sign any lease.

Moving In

Before your student occupies the apartment, they should do a walk-through of the rental with the landlord or their representative. The condition of the unit should be noted in writing either on the lease or an addendum (extra sheet of paper) attached to the lease. The notes should include anything of significance such as a large stain on the carpet or a door that was marred by the previous renter's pet. When your student moves out, they do not want to be charged for damage that was not their fault or existed prior to their moving in. Without documentation it's difficult to prove that the damage already existed. Your student should open every door, run the hot water, flush each toilet, turn on all appliances, and make sure everything works. It's also a good idea for them to record the state of the apartment when they move in using their cell phone to take pictures and video.

Renters insurance

After signing the lease, the next step is to buy renters insurance. While the landlord has insurance to rebuild or repair the apartment building, it protects the landlord's interest only. Your student needs insurance to protect his or her interest. The good news is that renters insurance is cheap, generally costing as little as $10 per month. It provides lots of protection for very little money. So what does a good renters insurance policy cover?

First, there should be enough to cover all of your student's personal property. Personal property includes furniture, clothing, electronics, computer, TV, and other personal items. Renters insurance will pay to replace all these items in the event of fire, theft, or other causes of loss (except flood). Without renters insurance your student is responsible for replacing everything they own in the event of loss.

Next, the policy should have adequate coverage for accidental damage and personal liability. Should your student accidentally cause damage to their or other units, renters insurance will cover the damages. With no renters insurance to protect you or your student, the landlord's insurance would pay for the damages to the unit, but then would come after your student if the damage was his or her fault. Legally, your student could be held responsible for all costs associated with the accident.

Just as important is personal liability coverage. Your student is responsible for anyone sustaining an injury while in their home or apartment. This responsibility would include medical expenses and attorneys' costs. Renters insurance provides protection for damages due to both accidents and instances where your student is held liable.

Finally, renters insurance should reimburse your student for additional living expenses due to any of the circumstances mentioned above. The smoke and water damage from that accidental grease fire could result in weeks of repair. During that time, where is your student going to stay? A good renters insurance policy should pay for their temporary housing for a couple of weeks.

But before you buy any renters insurance check your homeowners policy with your agent. In many instances your homeowners policy will extend to your student, particularly if they are living in a dorm.

Moving Out

Just as your student did his or her homework before moving in, there is homework to do before moving out. Your student was a good tenant. They made every payment on time and did not cause any damage to the unit. However, if the apartment is not in satisfactory condition, your student will not receive his or her full deposit back. So how can you and your student make sure the landlord gives back the full security deposit?

First, your student must leave the unit clean and in the same condition as when they first moved in. Vacuum and wipe the floors, clean the refrigerator and the oven, and scrub the bathrooms. Second, it's very important to do a walk-through with the landlord before they turn in the keys. This time it is up to the landlord to make sure everything still works and the apartment is in good condition. Your student should have the landlord indicate in writing that he or she has no further responsibility. Any damage that was there when your student moved in should have been noted in the lease. All your student needs to do is to call the landlord's attention to the lease or the addendum that they signed. Just as they did when they moved in, it is a good idea for them to take a video of the apartment when they move out.

It is essential that they give their landlord a forwarding address. Although their mail should automatically be forwarded, any packages that arrive from UPS or FedEx will not. Perhaps most important, your student's landlord will need a forwarding address so they know where to mail the security deposit refund.

On the whole, your student wants to move out in good standing. He or she may need the landlord as a reference for their next rental or on a mortgage or job application. Making payments on time, maintaining the apartment in good condition, and generally abiding by the rules could determine whether your student gets that next job or a new mortgage within a few years after graduation. Ultimately, the lessee/lessor relationship should be a pleasant and mutually beneficial one.

Living off-campus can provide your student their first experience of independence. It gives them the chance to experience all of the advantages and disadvantages of being responsible for their own welfare. As long as you and your student are diligent in doing your homework, understand the arrangements with roommates, and plan for all of the expenses, you and your student will make the right decision for his or her situation and personality.

Buying a Place

While this option is certainly not for everyone, it also is not just for the very wealthy. At first it may seem like overkill to buy a house for your student, but if your financial situation allows, buying a place may make good financial sense. In major metropolitan areas with sky-high housing prices this option probably will not work, but in many other college towns rental prices could make it a favorable investment.

Look for a two-bedroom or three-bedroom house or condominium. The idea is to rent the other rooms to other students. If you are in a market with low prices and low interest rates you can easily cover the mortgage payments with the rental income you will receive. While housing prices have dipped, rental costs have not, especially in college towns. College enrollment tends to remain steady or increase, so there is always a demand for student rental units.

This means your student could end up living off-campus for free. At the end of four years when your student graduates you may be able to sell the house for a small profit. If not, you could continue to rent the unit to other students until you are ready to sell.

You will have to decide if you really want to be a landlord and if your student will handle any of the responsibilities. If buying a place for your student sounds like something you want to research further there is plenty of information available on the Internet. There are also many good books on the subject. It is important to keep in mind that purchasing a place for your student to live is an investment and should be treated as such. As with any investment there is a chance you will earn money, but there is a chance you could lose money as well.

Chapter 5
Choose the Right Box:
Money Decisions

College is expensive. You want your student to get the most education for every dollar spent. So far we have discussed tuition and housing. There is little you can do to control the cost of tuition, other than those steps outlined earlier. There is also little you and your student can do to control the cost of housing other than choosing the best housing situation that fits your student's personality and college needs. The next step is to figure out what are all the *other* true costs associated with attending college. These are the costs that can be controlled. Only then can your student begin to minimize those costs and maximize their value of college.

Cars

Buying or owning a vehicle may be one of the most expensive items in your student's monthly budget. Unless you are going to make the payments, pay for the maintenance and insurance, and supply the gas, your student could be in for some real sticker shock. If your student does not currently own a car, then you will have to consider whether now is the best time for him or her to take on the responsibility of vehicle ownership. Certainly commuter students need to have a way to get to and from campus, but what about those living on-campus or in housing near campus? In fact, some colleges do not even allow new students to bring a car to campus during their freshman and sometimes even sophomore years.

Are Cars a Necessity?

In your student's situation, is car ownership really a necessity or is it a luxury? Do they really need a car at all? The real answer may be "no" if he or she is living on or near a campus with reliable public or student transportation. Many campuses are in fact designed to make car use impractical. Owning a car is more convenient than having to wait for the bus or subway, but how much are you and your student willing to pay for that convenience? In 2012 the IRS allowed you to deduct 55.5 cents for every mile driven for business purposes. This rate represents a fairly accurate overall cost to drive a car. You can use this to factor your student's anticipated vehicle expense. The costs of owning a car are extremely high and most students only need the car to get to their job. Ironically, they only need the job to pay for the car. Your student could save thousands by not owning a car while in college. Of course, if there is no public transportation, your student may have little choice but to own a vehicle.

Analyze Your Student's Needs

Since one of your goals is for your student to graduate with as little debt as possible, consider whether owning a car still fits within that goal. If your student already owns a car but determines it is not necessary during college, they could sell the car and apply those dollars toward college costs. Of course, be sure that they will not need the car during the summer. If so, perhaps it will cost less to leave the car at home and only use it during the summer.

Insurance rates will be lower if your student notifies their agent that they are "parking the car" for the semester.

If your student needs to have a car and they do not have one already, then they will soon be looking at purchasing a car. But there are many decisions. What type of car? Should they own a sports car, a hybrid, an SUV? Will it be new or used? Do you or your student have the cash to buy a car? How best should your student finance a car? What room is there in your student's budget for a car loan? Are they going to be struggling just to pay their bills or rent? Do they want to drive something decent or is a P.O.S. okay? (Of course, P.O.S. stands for Piece of Sheet metal.)

Most people do a poor job of making a wise car purchase. They begin by going to the car lot and looking at cars. They find a car first and then try to fit it into their budget. Your student should determine what they can afford first and then go find the car that fits their budget and meets their needs. This means they need to be clear on what kind of car they really need, what its true total cost of ownership is, and what is a fair price they should pay. It's not until all the research has been done that they set foot on the car lot to look at cars. By then your student will be armed with everything needed to buy the car that is right for them and not let the dealer talk them into a car that is more than they really require or can afford. For your student the car buying process begins with analyzing his or her needs.

It cannot be stressed strongly enough. This is where most people go wrong. They step onto a car lot, or even the Internet, and make an emotional decision to purchase the car. Then they go home and try to figure out how to afford the monthly payments. The smart way to purchase a car is to start by creating a budget and then determining exactly how much of the monthly budget surplus your student is willing to comfortably spend on his or her car.

Total Cost of Ownership

When your student creates his or her budget and tries to determine how much they can afford as a monthly car payment, they need to include a reasonable amount of money for car maintenance and insurance. It is expected that buying a new car will result in minimal maintenance costs, which is generally true. However, keep in mind that all cars have scheduled maintenance that needs to be done, and most of those costs begin after the warranty period expires, but before a five-year car loan is paid off. According to Edmunds.com, the average cost over five years for maintenance and repair of a brand new Honda Civic is almost $1,900, including nearly $800 in year four (based on recommended preventative maintenance), with similar types of cars having similar costs.[vi]

Automobile Insurance

All but one state requires drivers to carry some minimum level of automobile insurance. (New Hampshire is the only state that does not have compulsory auto insurance liability laws as of June 2010.[vii]) Yet the minimum required amounts do little to really protect you and your student from financial ruin. The problem is compounded by the complexity of automobile insurance terms, rules, and regulations. Automobile policies are difficult to understand, making it easy to overpay and underinsure if you're not careful.

Most people recognize car insurance by three numbers. For example, 30/60/25 is a common minimum insurance requirement in many states. But what do those numbers mean? The only number most people pay attention to is the number on the monthly or semiannual car insurance bill. A policy with 30/60/25 coverage provides $30,000 maximum payout to any one person for bodily injury from an accident, $60,000 maximum payout to all parties for bodily injury, and $25,000 maximum payout for property damage. That's really not a lot of coverage, especially when you consider it is only liability coverage. All that protection is for damage your student does to someone else. There is no coverage for damage to their car or property.

Better coverage is 100/300/50. The true purpose of insurance is protection from financial catastrophe. With the high cost of car repairs and hospital stays, 30/60/25 coverage is just not enough. Buying a policy with 100/300/50 coverage gives your student $100,000 per person or $300,000 per incident for bodily injury as well as up to $50,000 for property damage. Many experts agree that 100/300/50 coverage provides adequate protection in most cases.

So now that your student can cover damages they do to someone else, how do they protect their own property? Consider collision and comprehensive insurance. Unless their car is nothing more than a P.O.S., or piece of sheet metal, collision and comprehensive coverage is a must. In fact, all lenders will require your student to have collision and comprehensive if they have an outstanding loan on their car.

Collision coverage pays for damages to your student's car when it is involved in an accident. If your student wants it fixed without having to pay for the repairs out of his or her own pocket, they need collision coverage. Comprehensive coverage protects against loss from damage that is not related to a collision. This includes things such as fire, theft, vandalism, hailstorm, and the like. If a tree falls on your student's car while at the park, the comprehensive insurance will pay for the damages. If your student cannot afford to replace their car without financial heartburn, or if they have a car loan, they need collision and comprehensive insurance. And the greater the value of their car, the more coverage they need. However, if their car is older and has little value, it may make sense to drop collision and comprehensive coverage.

To understand that last point it helps to understand how insurance companies compensate drivers for any damage. If your student wrecks a 10-year-old car worth $2,500 and it costs $4,000 to fix the car, the insurance company will give them a check for $2,500 less the deductible and consider the car "totaled." Often, it doesn't take a lot of damage to an older or less expensive car for it to be considered totaled. Most insurance companies consider the car totaled once the repairs reach 80% of replacement cost, while some will total the car when they are just 51% of the replacement value.[viii]

Bottom line is that cars are expensive. They are expensive to buy, they are expensive to maintain, they are expensive to finance, and they are expensive to insure. Cars can be a huge budget buster for a college student.

Small Money Decisions

Most students and parents worry about the rising costs of tuition and stress over making the tuition payment each semester. But when you break it down, for most students and especially for in-state students, the tuition bill is the smallest and easiest part of paying for college. At one university on the east coast, in-state tuition per semester is $1,440. Fees are an additional $958, almost doubling the tuition. Room rates for on-campus housing average around $2,300 and meal plans are over $1,500. Add in $373 for student health insurance and the bill for one semester totals $6,571. Tuition represented less than 1/4 of the total cost.

Now, throw in $700 for dining out and snacks (yes, this is for on-campus students), another $600 for books, and $700 for personal expenses and students pay more than $8,500 per semester. What if they purchase a car while going to college? In addition to the $100 parking pass, they need about $600 for car insurance and about $3,000 for other vehicle costs including the car payment, maintenance, and gasoline.

At the end of the semester an in-state student who owns a car and lives on campus can expect to spend over $12,200. Suddenly the tuition bill seems like peanuts compared to everything else. And tuition is something you or your student cannot control. To really keep costs down, it is better to focus on expenses that you and your student can control.

Textbooks

It is easy to spend more than $1,000 per year on textbooks, sometimes even in a single semester. However, there are some cheaper options for purchasing textbooks than just going to the campus bookstore. Books can be purchased online through chegg.com, craigslist.org, half.com and Campus Book Swap. Tell your student to consider purchasing electronic textbooks if possible. In some instances, E-books can cut textbook costs in half.

There are even some free textbooks. Textbook/Media Press (www.textbookmedia.com) offers a number of electronic texts. The downside is that they include advertisements within the books. Other sites, such as Bartleby.com offer classic literature that can be downloaded for free.

Also, tell your student to consider sharing books with classmates or see if a library copy is available. At first you may hesitate to make such a recommendation, but consider the side benefits of this approach. Your student might learn to be more efficient with his or her time because they will have to be disciplined enough to plan their work to accommodate everyone using the book.

Another option that is gaining popularity is textbook rental. Many university bookstores offer a limited selection of textbooks that can be rented for the semester. Online websites such as chegg.com offer a much larger selection. Sometimes for less than half the price of buying a textbook, your student can rent one for the semester as long as they return it in useable condition.

Your student may consider attending the first day of class before purchasing the textbook. Sometimes a book is listed as required or recommended for a course, but the instructor will let students know on the first day whether or not the book is essential. In some instances a prior edition of the text will work for the course, which could save your student some money.

Your student should sell nonessential books when the semester is over. And there are places besides the campus bookstore to sell used textbooks. To get the most for their used books, your student should handle the books with care and with as few marks as possible. Textbooks are updated frequently with new editions released every one to two years. Your student will have better luck selling their books if they act quickly after classes are over.

Little Things Add Up

There are many other costs that, although they are not directly related to education, must be taken into consideration as well. Some are unavoidable, whereas others are a lifestyle choice. Just the bare necessity of food can be a major cost that many families and students fail to incorporate into the student's budget. Many colleges have a variety of meal plans available to your student, whether they are a commuter or living on campus. However, even with a meal plan, they are going to want snacks and drinks on hand and want to dine out from time to time. Certainly, you have to consider clothing expenses as well. Every college student wants the occasional T-shirt and sweatshirt bearing their school colors and logo.

Of course, there will be some expenses that cannot be predicted but will need to be included. Students who move far from home may need money set aside for travel as they visit home over holidays, vacations, and breaks. In addition, many students and their parents experience sticker shock from the increased costs associated with living in a more expensive city. Finally, do not overlook or underestimate the cost of entertainment and other miscellaneous expenses.

Even though students are typically in good health, most parents and students underestimate health-care expenses while in college, including the cost for health insurance. Many colleges now require that students either buy health insurance from the college's provider or prove that they have coverage from another plan. In fact, many colleges have a hard waiver policy, which means your student is automatically covered and charged for health insurance. Always be sure to check for a health insurance charge on the tuition bill. If the school has a hard waiver policy for health insurance, and your student is already covered by your plan, then submit the waiver and save several hundred dollars. The financial aid and the cashier's offices can provide details.

Finally, you and your student might consider shopping secondhand for inexpensive or free stuff that they need or want while in college. Secondhand furniture is much less expensive than new items. Anyone can find desks, tables, dressers, couches, chairs, lamps, reconditioned appliances, and rugs at local garage sales, flea markets, and charity shops. It's easy to search for used items online or in the classified section of the local newspaper. While online, they can download the latest open source software to save on expensive software. For example, the OpenOffice suite (www.openoffice.org) is a great alternative to Microsoft's Office Suite and is absolutely free. At the very least, check with your campus bookstore for software as many campuses offer students steep discounts on student versions of popular software.

More Quarters in the Couch

When we talk about finding more quarters in the couch we really are talking about finding money that is already there, but your student just doesn't know it. Like the $10 bill they find in the pocket of a pair of pants, it was always there; they just didn't realize it until they stuck their hand in the pocket. Most budgets have lots of "pockets", many of them full of ten dollar bills. Your student just needs to look around. Otherwise, they end up like most people and focus on making more money. Lots of students work part-time or even second jobs to bolster their budget. However, if they would just spend some of that energy on properly directing and controlling their spending they would be much further ahead financially.

Let's look at several easy ways for your college student to take control of their spending while in college.

Dining Out

One of the deepest and fullest pockets in your student's budget is dining out. It's not just going out to dinner once in a while, but all the quick little dashes into the convenience store they need to watch.

Gourmet coffees, energy drinks, and power smoothies cost your student hundreds of dollars each semester if not each month. The problem is that most students do not see $3 - $6 per drink as a lot of money, but when you add them up over a month's time they become a big budget buster. The innocent $6.00 Starbucks™ coffee when purchased just twice a week adds up to over $624 a year. Buy one every day and it costs over $1,560 a year. Instead, recommend they opt for one gourmet treat per week, or buy them in bulk at Target or Wal-Mart and grab one from their own refrigerator each day.

And that is just the coffee part of their day. Add in a few fast food lunches two to three times per week instead of brown bagging it. A sub with chips and a drink is almost $10. That will easily cost your student over $1,300 a year. Food brought from home (or their apartment) is almost free since they already paid for it.

Even water costs more than $1 per bottle. If your student buys just three bottles per week they end up spending more than $150 per year. Instead, buy them a refillable water bottle. Not only will they save money, but they will also help the environment by using fewer disposable plastic bottles.

Lots of money is spent needlessly for convenience when a little effort could save an awful lot of money each month and each year. Dining out eats up their paycheck, their financial aid, and any money they get from you. It is death by a thousand little cuts and most students never even realize they are getting nicked.

Personal Expenses

Many parents and students are surprised by how much small personal expenses add up while at college. Cutting each expense just a little can add up to big savings over the time it takes your student to earn his or her degree.

Most students and parents often underestimate the cost of social life while at college. Restaurant, bar, and theater expenses eat up a lot of money. Yet, it is not that hard for your student to socialize on a budget. It's easy if they take advantage of free on-campus concerts, movies, or other events provided by student unions and other campus organizations. They can check out local museums or art galleries as well as nature parks for hiking. In addition, many local businesses and parks offer student discounts, but it is up to your student to ask for them.

Buy Bulk

Buying in bulk is not just for large families but for college students too, especially those who live off-campus. When it comes to non-perishable items, everyone can save by buying in bulk. While it may seem silly on the surface for your student to buy 36 rolls of toilet paper or 18 rolls of paper towels, the price break adds up over time. While it may initially be a strain on the budget to make that lump sum purchase, the lower price per quantity will pay dividends to their budget in the months ahead. If done properly over time, they will have the money for bulk purchases as they go four, six, or even eight months without having to buy some of these items.

A word of caution is warranted concerning large shopping clubs. Discount warehouses such as Sam's Club™ or Costco™ can save your student a lot of money if they are careful, but not all bulk items are a good deal. If you have ever been to one of these shopping clubs you know they carry unusual sizes. While your student may be able to estimate what they pay for an item of a certain size at Wal-Mart™ or the grocery store, that size usually can't be found at the discount warehouse. It can be hard to discern a bargain if they are not shopping price per quantity. If not careful, they could easily be overpaying based on price per quantity and think they are getting a bargain because they are buying in bulk.

Buy Value

One of the best ways to become a smarter consumer is to get the best value on every purchase.

A great way to add value on purchases is to clip coupons. Some people think coupons are worthless, but it is easy to save at least $10 per trip to the grocery store using coupons. In addition to groceries, your student can save money on pizza, oil changes, and more. There is a coupon to save on almost everything. It really does not take much time nor is it inconvenient. They just need to make sure they use coupons only for items they were going to buy anyway. If a coupon entices them to buy something for which they have not budgeted or need, then they have succumbed to the marketing and spent more money, not less.

The following are some great ways for your student to cut costs.

- Buy store brands of food instead of name brands.
- Buy items on sale. Check a few different advertisements of nearby grocery stores and compare.
- Don't make large purchases until they think about it for at least a week.
- They should make a list of things they need and only buy what is on their list.
- They can drop their landline phone if possible, or eliminate extras such as call waiting and caller ID.
- Do they really need 105 channels? They can reduce their cable bill to the basic tier or eliminate it completely.
- They can pack their lunch instead of dining out. If they buy their lunch every day at $8 per day, they spend over $160 every month on food (that's more than $1,900 per year!). Most people can usually pack for about $60 per month or less (that's a $1,200 savings per year).
- They can make their own coffee in the morning; they don't need to pay $3 for a super fancy brew every day. That's another $60 per month they are spending.
- They can avoid extended service plans when they purchase an electronic gadget or an appliance. The plans are overpriced.

As your student begins to understand the big picture of why they are in college and what steps they can take to be successful, they will start to get really excited about the whole process. Once they see that there are ways to reduce their expenses and keep their costs low, they will be better equipped to focus on making college a successful experience and less focused on worrying about their financial situation. However, most students will quickly realize they simply do not have enough cash to cover all of their college expenses and will need to look for the best ways to pay for college.

Chapter 6
Think Outside the Box:
How to Pay for College

College is expensive. Since your goal is to help your student avoid moving back home after college, it is important to pay for college the right way. So what is the best way to go about paying for college? The truth is most families use a combination of ways to pay for school, including grants, scholarships, family, jobs, and even loans. Which ones are best? Unfortunately, most parents and students choose the most harmful ways more often than not.

How can you know what the best combination is for you and your student? First let's learn some terms. Some people use the terms aid, grants, and scholarships interchangeably. Financial aid includes the total package of assistance which can include grants (free money), scholarships (free money), and loans (money that has to be paid back). It is important to understand these terms when discussing or reviewing your student's total financial aid package. It is crucial to know which dollars must be repaid and which do not. Now we can discuss your options and the process and then look at the best to worst ways to pay for college.

The FAFSA

The very first step in determining how to pay for college is filling out and submitting the FAFSA (Free Application for Federal Student Aid). The FAFSA can be completed in paper form or can be submitted by phone, but the easiest way to complete the form is online at www.fafsa.ed.gov. This is a free application. No one or no website should ever ask for any kind of fee.

All federal and state financial aid and almost all other financial aid programs use the FAFSA to determine eligibility. It is important to complete the application early, accurately, and completely. The FAFSA can be filed as early as January 1st for the fall semester, and must be submitted each year. Each college has somewhat different filing deadlines. You and your student should meet with the school's financial aid office or at least visit their website to understand the rules, regulations, and deadlines to ensure that his or her financial aid is in place to cover the tuition bill when it comes due.

Steps to Federal Student Aid[ix]

The application process is not difficult, but it is not completely painless. Both you and your student need to gather some basic information such as Social Security numbers, birth dates, and tax returns before beginning the application. Once the FAFSA is completed your student will receive a SAR or Student Aid Report. The SAR summarizes the information included on the FAFSA and provides the EFC (Expected Family Contribution) that colleges use to determine the financial aid package.

Next, the college financial aid office determines the type and amount of aid options available to your student for which he or she qualifies. The information that you and your student receives at this point does not necessarily represent the best way to pay for college, only what you and your student are eligible to receive through the college. The financial aid office will explain eligibility for grants, scholarships, and loans, but it is really up to you and your student to determine the best combination of options.

In the financial aid world, the term "financial need" usually does not reflect true need. It is based on how much the college is expected to cost minus the amount of money you and your student are expected to contribute toward that cost. In financial aid terms, it is the cost of attendance (determined by the school) minus the Expected Family Contribution (EFC) as determined by the FAFSA. The school's cost of attendance includes tuition and fees, room and board, books and supplies, transportation, personal expenses, and even student loan fees. The EFC is based on a formula set by the Department of Education and uses both your and your student's contributions from assets (the things that both you and your student own) plus your and your student's contributions from income (how much both you and your student earn).

Cost of Attendance

Almost all students earning their first undergraduate degree are considered dependent on their parents, at least according to the Department of Education. Even if your student is completely on their own, they still have to include your information on the FAFSA. The federal government assumes that if a student is under 24 years of age, Mom and Dad have the primary responsibility of paying for their undergraduate education.[x] Only in unusual circumstances is a student considered independent for purposes of the FAFSA if they are less than 24 years old.[xi]

Of course, it's almost impossible to fully represent your particular situation in numbers and forms. If your student has a special situation or something unexpected happens, they should talk to their financial aid counselor first and certainly before they take any action or make any decision. They should never withdraw from college for financial reasons without first speaking to their financial aid counselor. The financial aid office is there to help. They can use their professional judgment to help your student, but only if your student lets them know what unique situation they are facing. A financial aid counselor should be one of your student's first friends on campus. They will do whatever is within their power to help.

Of all the multitude of ways to pay for college some are much better than others. Let's begin with the best ways (free money) and work down to the least desirable ways (money that has to be paid back).

Grants

Finding and applying for grants should be the first place to look for financial aid because grant money is like a gift and does not need to be repaid. Most grants come from the state and federal government, such as the Pell Grant and the Supplemental Educational Opportunity Grant. However, there are also college-specific and private grants. Most grants are need-based with eligibility determined by the FAFSA.

Your student does not have to repay grant money as long as they remain in good standing and are successfully progressing in the completion of their degree. Failing to meet all the requirements of the grant could result in having to pay it back. Typically this includes dropping below a minimum GPA, withdrawing before the end of the semester, or failing to maintain full-time or half-time status. Some grant requirements are determined by the college or university and vary from school to school. It is very important to apply before all deadlines. Applications submitted after the posted deadlines are rejected.

There are a large number of federal, state, and private grants available for students. The most common federal grants include the Federal Pell Grant, the Federal Supplemental Educational Opportunity Grant (FSEOG), Teacher Education Assistance for College and Higher Education Grant (TEACH Grant), and even the Iraq and Afghanistan Service Grant. Each grant has its own criteria for eligibility. You can find out more at www.studentaid.ed.gov and the school's financial aid office.

There are other institutional grants in addition to the ones from the federal government. Some are merit based and are awarded for high academic achievement. Others are need based, either on your finances or those of your student. Many of these types of grants come with specific obligations. When taking any grant money remember that if your student does not maintain eligibility they may have to pay it back. It is "free" money only so long as they hold up their end of the deal. They should ask their financial aid office for any institutional grants specific to the school and the state they live in.

Scholarships

Like grants, scholarships typically do not require repayment as long as your student maintains eligibility. Many are need based, but there are also scholarships that center on specific criteria such as academics, athletics, community service, the arts, or a whole host of other things. The scholarships can be from their university, their major or program, private donors, or other organizations. There are scholarships for bringing a specific talent to the school, such as athletics, music, or the performing arts. There are state-sponsored scholarships, scholarships for students whose parents work for particular companies, and scholarships sponsored by churches or civic organizations.

It's important to be persistent in finding scholarships. Sometimes all it takes is to apply. Your student just needs to complete the application or interview by the deadline. The tricky part is finding them. The two best places to find scholarships are the financial aid office and the Internet. A financial aid counselor can point them to specific scholarships offered from their state or their school. Studentaid.ed.gov and fastweb.com are great websites with links to numerous scholarships. Finally, many scholarships from small local organizations in your hometown may not show up in any database. Even if your student is already in college, their former high school may still be the best source of information on local scholarships.

Scholarships have very early deadlines and come with strings attached. Some deadlines can be as far as a year in advance. If your student fails to maintain eligibility they may lose the scholarship and be forced to pay it back. If for example, they cannot play their sport, they would lose their athletic scholarship, or if their GPA falls, they would lose their academic scholarship. You and your student need to fully understand the ongoing requirements of the scholarship so they do not lose it or are not forced to pay it back.

It is unnecessary for you to pay someone to help you and your student search for grants or scholarships. The financial aid counselor is already paid by the college to provide assistance. In addition, there are plenty of free resources on the Internet to help you and your student find grants and scholarships.

Tax Credits

Tax credits can save you and your student thousands of dollars by reducing your tax bill at the end of the year. Although tax credits are not thought of as financial aid in the traditional sense, it can mean additional money to help pay for school. Any money not paid in taxes is money that can be used to pay for tuition, books, or meals.

The American Opportunity Credit can reduce your tax expense by up to a maximum of $2,500 per student per year. Likewise, the Lifetime Learning Credit can lower your tax expense by up to $2,000 per year for each child you have in college, or for your student up to $2,000 per year. There is no limit on the number of years the Lifetime Learning Credit can be claimed. However, the American Opportunity Credit and Lifetime Learning Credit cannot both be claimed for the same student in the same year.[xii] The important point is that although you and your student are entitled to one or more tax credits, you have to ask for it on your tax returns. It is not automatic.

A few states also offer state tax credits for tuition expenses. The best place to start is to search your state's department of higher education website to determine if your state offers any educational tax credits.

Pay As You Go

After finding all the free money you can (grants, scholarships, and even tax credits), the next best way to pay for college is for your student to work. Make no mistake; college is hard. That is why more than a third of students never earn their degree. However, it is possible for your student to find an appropriate balance between school and work while still earning good grades.

Earning their own money goes a long way in establishing your student's independence, building their self-esteem, and gaining valuable work experience. Plus it helps pay a few college bills at the same time. However, some jobs are better than others. The best part-time jobs pay well, provide career related experience, and are flexible around class schedules. Let's start with work study.

Work Study

Federal College Work Study is one of the most overlooked forms of financial aid available. Your student works for the college or university but is paid with federal financial aid dollars. This is different from being a university employee and being paid with university dollars. Federal work study is part of federal financial aid.

There are several advantages to work study. First, work study earnings do not impact your student's eligibility for financial aid the following year. If your student works a part-time job off campus they have to include those earnings on their next year's FAFSA, and it is used in determining total expected family contribution. Second, your student gets to learn new skills and gain experience, which they can include on their resume. Third, because they are working at their university, their supervisor tends to be more flexible when it comes to working around their class schedule.

While your student's school may offer work study as a part of their financial aid package, they are not required to accept this portion if they do not have time to work. However, any work study financial aid that they accept is money they do not have to borrow. Plus, if they must work to pay for college, work study is one of the best jobs they can choose because of all the advantages.

It is important for your student to let the financial aid office know they want work study. Funding is limited, and the school wants to make sure the money is there for students who do want to work.

Cooperative Education

The next best thing to work study is cooperative education (co-op). Many schools and departments offer paid co-op programs. These are typically available regardless of whether or not your student qualifies for a work study position. The best co-op jobs are paid and are related to their major. They might consider an unpaid co-op job for the experience and job contacts, but if their goal is to finance college then they should only consider paid co-op positions. In addition, many co-op jobs pay higher wages than work study jobs. Your student should talk to their career services office and their advisor to find co-op jobs that are best suited for their circumstances.

Good Deeds

A number of not-for-profit agencies offer some sort of tuition reimbursement or forgiveness program in exchange for your student's commitment to work with them for some length of time after graduation. AmeriCorps, Peace Corps, and Teach for America all offer educational service awards that help pay for school while they do something that makes a difference in the world. Unlike scholarships and grants, a service award from one of these organizations usually does not affect federal financial aid eligibility.

That is the good news. However, most of these programs require that your student successfully complete one or two years of service before any money is received. The money must be used to pay for costs related to obtaining his or her degree or to repay his or her school loans.

Other groups to check out include the National Health Service Corps, the Army National Guard, and the National Institutes of Health. Each of these have student loan forgiveness programs that help pay off school loans in exchange for going to work for them for a year or more after graduation. Volunteers in Service to America (VISTA) and the Reserve Officers Training Corps (ROTC) not only have these programs, but also have programs that provide cash while in school if your student commits to some service time immediately after graduation. Each group has a good website with details on their specific program.

Get Paid to Live on Campus

Living off campus is usually cheaper than living on campus. Here is the exception. Your student can become a resident assistant (RA) or resident director (RD). If they keep their grades up and stay out of trouble, after their freshman year they can apply to be an RA or an RD. Generally, they live in the residence hall for free (or at reduced cost) and work by being on call or planning and organizing activities for their residence hall. In addition to a free room, other perks can include free meal plans, a stipend (paycheck), and even the obligatory free T-shirt. It is a job that allows your student to put their academics first, plus they get to develop leadership, facilitation, management, and team-building skills that enhance their resume.

Get a Real Job

After you and your student exhaust all the grant, scholarship, and on-campus job opportunities, your student may still need additional money to help pay for college. Working a part-time job could be the final piece of this puzzle. A part-time job is a great way to close the gap if your student is a little cash strapped. Plus, if they do it right, a part-time job can give them valuable job experience they can add to their resume. They should look for a part-time job that is related to their major, or even better, with the company they would like to work for after they graduate. Students that work part-time for a company during college are that company's prime job candidates once they finish their degrees.

What your student has to guard against is letting the part-time job negatively affect their grades. Ultimately, it is up to them to balance the demands of their studies with the demands of their job. They should build their job schedule around their class schedule, not the other way around. They should always prioritize their studies over their job. The key is to balance their job with their course work. If they do it well, they will have extra money in their pocket as well as hands-on experience that will be invaluable to them.

Although part-time jobs can be beneficial, it is **not** recommend that your student work full-time while trying to attend school full-time. Rarely does this work out well. The added stress of working full-time while in college is immense. It is better to find some other solution so that your student can focus on their school work, even if it means taking out a student loan.

Parents and Family

Only after you and your student have exhausted all grant and scholarship opportunities, and your student is working part-time, should you start using your money to help. Certainly, it is okay at this point to use your money, but it needs to be done the right way. Remember, the government expects you to help your student pay for college as long as they are less than 24 years old or are considered a dependent. Most parents will do almost anything to make sure their student has the money to go to school. Yet almost no parent has the expertise to navigate the financial aid minefield. This means parents and families often make very poor financial decisions when it comes to paying for college.

Just as there are good and bad options for your student to pay for college, there are good and bad options for you to help them pay for college as well. You should not spend all your money and savings on your student's college education. Otherwise, there may be a day in the future when they have to take care of you. If you spend your retirement account to send your student to college, you may have to move in with them later in life. No one wants that. Just as important, you should avoid doing something with your money that would result in less financial aid to your student. So what do you need to know about financial aid to best help your student?

Early Birds

Start planning early. Student financial aid is based on a combination of your and your student's previous year's income and assets for each year you apply for financial aid. It is important to plan early each year so that everybody can put their money in the right place to make sure your student gets the most financial aid possible. In the college financial aid world, the early bird gets the check.

Whose Money Is It Anyway?

As a general rule, it is better to keep any savings and any income in your name rather than in your student's name whenever possible. In the financial aid or needs analysis formulas, certain types of incomes and assets count more than others. Typically, income and assets included in your student's name count against them more than if it is in your name.

In addition, it is critically important to carefully read the instructions on how to complete the FAFSA. It gets really technical, but certain assets, such as retirement accounts, do not have to be included so they will not count against your student's financial aid. The mistake of including an asset when it should not be included can result in a lot less financial aid, particularly the free kind.

This next part your student will love; you not so much. Income in your student's name counts more against the amount of financial aid awarded than income in your name. Many financial aid experts advise that if at all possible students should try to keep their annual income from any job other than work study to $3,700 or less. This gives your student the greatest chance of maximizing their financial aid award.

Retirement or College

It is a very bad idea for you to borrow against or take money out of your retirement accounts to pay for your student to attend college.

It may also be a bad idea to skip putting money into your retirement accounts while your student is attending college and use that money for their college expenses.

Retirement funds are special tax-sheltered accounts. If you stop contributing for a few years, you cannot go back and add that money in later since there are certain limits to the amount of money you can contribute each year. If you take money from these accounts before you are supposed to you pay income tax on the withdrawals. On top of that, you pay a penalty unless you can clearly prove that the money paid for a qualifying educational expense. You would be lucky to keep two-thirds of what you withdraw to pay for your student to attend college. Even if you simply borrow against the account, all the aforementioned penalties would still apply if you lose or quit your job before the loan is paid back.

In addition, retirement accounts are not included in the financial aid formulas. However, if you take the money out of your retirement account and put it in a regular savings or checking account, or even worse give it to your student, it counts in the financial aid formula and reduces their financial aid award. Taking money out of your retirement account is one of the worst ways for you to help your student pay for college.

Home Equity Loans

If you do not qualify for a federal student loan you may consider a home equity loan. Equity is the difference between the value of your home and what you owe on it. Home equity loans often have lower interest rates than loans from private lenders and certainly lower rates than credit cards. Plus the interest paid on a home equity loan is usually tax deductible. Keep in mind that a home equity loan is still a loan, and it does cost interest. Plus, interest rates for home equity loans usually vary with economic conditions and can be higher than federal student loan interest rates.

The biggest mistake you could make with a home equity loan is to put the amount borrowed in a checking or savings account. It would then be included in the expected family contribution and count against your student in the financial aid formula. It's always best to see if your student qualifies for a federal student loan first. Home equity loans should be one of the last resorts to help pay for your student's college.

PLUS Loan for Parents

You may also apply for a federal loan to help pay for your student's educational expenses. PLUS loans are available to you if you are the biological, adoptive, or step parent and if you have an acceptable credit report. You must complete the FAFSA, a PLUS loan application, and sign a master promissory note (MPN). You need to sign only one MPN for as long as your student is in school. The school will use the PLUS loan to pay for tuition, fees, room and board, and any other school expenses first. Anything left over is sent to you in the form of a check or direct deposit. Note that you may choose not to accept any leftover money and instead use it to reduce the total amount of your loan.

It is important to recognize that a relatively high interest rate of 7.9% for PLUS loans was set many years ago and is paid on the loan from the date of the first check. More important, PLUS loans also charge a fee of 4% each time a disbursement is made. Yes, that's right, 4% is deducted from the PLUS loan check each time financial aid is disbursed. Are you beginning to see why loans are one of the worst options to help pay for college?

Private Student Loans for Parents

Private student loans can be very tempting. Most parents will do almost anything to make sure their student can go to college. Private student loan companies can give almost instant approval using quick, easy-to-use online forms. However, they usually have much less favorable repayment terms and higher interest rates than federal loans. In addition, unlike federal loans, private student loans are based on your credit score, so your credit report must be pristine. If your credit score is questionable, you may wind up with a loan that has less-than-favorable terms. Some even have variable interest rates that reset monthly. Private student loans are one of the worst possible ways to finance your student's college education.

Some parents borrow money for their student with the expectation that the student will help them repay those loans after they graduate and start working. While not a pleasant topic to discuss, for your financial protection, you should carry enough life insurance on your student to pay off those loans should something tragic happen. Unfortunately, particularly with private student loans and home equity loans, if you personally signed or cosigned for the loans, the lenders will come after you for the full amount.

Grandparents

Do not forget about your parents. Grandparents want to help your student get a college degree too. Even if they do not have any money they can still help pay for college in many ways. Many students are eligible for scholarships based on their grandparents' affiliations such as Kiwanis, Lions Club, United Auto Workers, and other organizations. Your student should ask their grandparents to provide them with a list of all their affiliations, including past and present employers, unions, military service, memberships, hobbies, and other activities. Your student can begin by looking for legacy scholarships, military scholarships, and scholarships based on ancestry and ethnicity.

Bottom Line

The bottom line is that your student's financial aid award is dependent on both your and your student's financial picture. The whole family will need to work together to present the best picture to the school's financial aid office so that your student gets not just the most, but the best type of financial aid available.

Student Loans

Finally, there are student loans. While most students and families seek out student loans as their first choice to pay for college, we intentionally listed student loans as the last choice as a way to pay for a college education. That is because student loans have a greater impact on your student's long-term financial health than any other financial aid they can use. In 2010, total student loan debt surpassed total credit card debt for the first time.[xiii] Most students and parents do not realize how much they are borrowing for college or how big the student's payments will be after they graduate.

Yes, students have to begin paying back their student loans very soon after graduation. The more money they borrow, the larger their student loan payment will be. The larger their student loan payment is, the less money they have available to spend on other things. The point is that student loan debt takes away their choices. That $250 per month payment they make on their student loans is $250 they cannot spend on rent, food, a car, and other personal choices.

Yet most students still have to use student loans to help pay for their college education. As much as you want to discourage your student from taking out student loans, if they have to choose between borrowing money and not going to college, then by all means they should borrow the money. They should not borrow the money to finance their spring break or other luxuries. Too many students view student loans simply as "free money", without ever giving thought to what it will take to pay them back. Earning a college degree is the single most valuable action they can take to ensure their long-term personal financial health, so they should not be afraid to make the investment. However, it's important that your student knows what the impact of their student loans will be. Let's begin with the most borrower-friendly student loans available and work our way to the least.

Perkins Loan

A Perkins Loan is a relatively low 5% interest loan your student can apply for through their school's financial aid office. The money comes from government funds, but they borrow from their school and they pay their school back after they graduate. If they demonstrate exceptional financial need, they can borrow up to $5,500 per year and pay it back at the 5% interest rate. The amount they get depends on when they apply, their financial need, and the funds the school has at its disposal. Once the money runs out at their school, there is no more to award. It is important your student applies early to be awarded a Perkins loan. They must begin to pay this loan back nine months after they either graduate, drop below half-time, or leave school altogether.

Stafford Loan

Stafford loans are low interest loans where your student borrows directly from Uncle Sam; specifically the U.S. Department of Education. There are subsidized and unsubsidized loans, and it is important to understand the distinction between the two.

Subsidized loans are need-based, and the school determines how much your student will get after reviewing the FAFSA. Your student is not charged interest while in school or during the grace period after they graduate. (Uncle Sam pays for the interest or "subsidizes" this loan while they are in school.)

Unsubsidized loans do not require your student to demonstrate financial need. Like the subsidized loans, the school determines how much your student gets. However, unlike the subsidized loans, unsubsidized loans start charging interest from the moment the money is available to them. They get the option of paying just the interest while in school or deferring it until after they graduate. Of course, waiting until after they graduate to pay the interest increases their loan amount and their monthly payment.

Your student could qualify to get both a subsidized and an unsubsidized loan in the same year. If their subsidized loan does not cover all their expenses, they may be able to get an unsubsidized loan to cover the rest up to the maximum annual borrowing limit. As with all federal financial aid, you must complete the FAFSA first so the school can determine the amount of loan your student will receive. The Stafford loan is included as part of your student's total financial aid package and they have the option of accepting or rejecting any loans in that package.

Your student is required to sign a master promissory note (MPN) the first time they accept a Stafford loan. The MPN is the legal contract where they promise to repay the student loan to the Department of Education. It spells out in excruciating detail all the terms and conditions of the loan. In most cases they need to sign only one MPN for all their Stafford student loans while they are in school. Their school can give them a copy of an MPN or they can complete one online at studentloans.gov.

Private Student Loans

No discussion of student loans would be complete without talking about private or alternative loans. These are available from a variety of sources ranging from well-known and reputable banks and credit unions to less-than-reputable private loan sources. The terms of these loans vary by lender, but all are credit-based, have high and sometimes variable interest rates, and typically require a cosigner. Unfortunately, there are also many scam artists out there. The best advice is for you and your student to be very cautious when considering private educational loans. Federal student loans are the best alternative. Anyone considering a private student loan should first speak with the financial aid office at their school to see if they can help find one with good terms.

Tuition Payment Options

Unfortunately, even after looking under every rock for grants, scholarships, jobs, and loans, your student may still be a little short on tuition money. Fortunately, most colleges have a number of tuition payment options available, including monthly installment plans or payments. The point is that even after accepting all the financial aid, if your student is still unable to pay the balance of the tuition, there are options. Always talk to the financial aid office. Chances are the school offers a plan that will let you or your student spread out the balance of the tuition bill over a number of months or years.

Keep in mind that there is almost always some sort of fee or interest charged for deferment or extended or installment payment plans. It is your and your student's responsibilities to understand all the terms and requirements of any contract. However, it is always better for your student to stay in school, graduate with his or her degree, and owe a little extra interest, than to not graduate at all.

Why Avoid Debt?

Why can debt be such a problem? Your student is spending tomorrow's income...today. Debt carries with it an obligation to make those future payments. Your student makes a commitment to use their future income to pay off the debt. In addition, not only do they sacrifice future income, but they also pay more for everything when the interest charges are included. Everything becomes more expensive because they pay for the privilege to use someone else's money to buy the things they absolutely must have today. Finally, there are the opportunity costs. Money spent making payments is money not available to save, spend on an apartment, or help them reach their financial goals.

But borrowing money lets your student have things they want today, such as an education, while spreading the payments over a long period of time. Why should your student avoid debt? Or more important, why should your student avoid excessive debt? It's about choices. Everyone likes choices. And debt, especially student loan debt, will take away their choices. Let's look at an example.

Your student graduates and earns $36,000 per year and has a $400 car payment, $300 student loan payment, and a $200 credit card payment. They bring home around $2,000 per month after taxes, so even if rent is $600 your student is still okay with $500 per month to spend on food, gas, and so forth. Now, some life change happens. Maybe they want to change careers to do something they love or go to graduate school and only work part-time. In either case, assume their income will be lower and their take-home pay would drop to $1,500 per month.

Guess what? They can't make the change. They are stuck because of all of that debt. They cannot afford to pay for rent, along with food and utilities after making payments on their car, student loans, and credit card. There is just not enough left over. Suddenly, their money controls them, instead of them controlling their money. Their debt has limited their choices.

Debt Takes Away Choices

As illustrated time and again, debt takes away your student's choices. While they can use debt to leverage some positive things in their life such as buying a home or paying for a college education, the payments still take away some of their choices. If they truly want financial independence and they want to have as many choices as possible, then they should look for ways to minimize the amount of their debt. Money cannot buy happiness, but having a large positive cash flow in their budget each month after they graduate will certainly give them choices.

Now you and your student have had a chance to consider all the various ways to pay for college and how to keep costs to a minimum. Ultimately, as your student learns more about his or her personal finances and begins to employ tools such as a budget to control their finances, they will make fewer and fewer unnecessary purchases. Your student may be dealing with large amounts of money over the next several years in the form of paychecks from part-time jobs, student loan reimbursements, or other sources. To best handle these large sums (and even the smaller ones) they need to utilize a simple college budget. A budget lets them see where their money goes and, when it comes to their spending, lets them focus on those things that they can control.

Chapter 7
Handle with Care:
The College Budget

Yes, the word budget is going to be used – a lot. But budget is not a dirty word. Budgets are about money. Money is fun! Spending money is even more fun. Let's face it. Nobody updates their Facebook™ page with a status about saving money (Just put $20 into my emergency fund!). However, people always post about spending money (Just bought a new car; got the cutest shoes; took the coolest vacation). So here is the question. Has anyone ever taught your student how to spend the right way?

Whether your student has money coming from scholarships, a summer job, a part-time job during the semester, or even money from you, they are responsible for managing that money themselves. The easiest way for them to do this is to create a budget. Before they (or you) run away screaming, let's discuss why most people cringe at the word budget. They think budgets exist to take away all their fun. However, there is nothing painful about a budget. It is not some restrictive money diet that prevents you from spending money on what you really want. In fact, it does quite the opposite. A budget gives you the knowledge to spend your money on what you want and alleviates the stress of doing so.

So, why are some people so apprehensive about budgets? Numbers don't lie. One thing a budget will do is show you where you spend your money. It will shine a big light on all your spending habits. Many times there is a big difference between how you think you spend your money and how you actually spend your money. It is this difference that makes some people uncomfortable with budgets. The good news is that narrowing this gap empowers you to take control of your financial life. This is a budget's greatest strength.

Budget sheets show you how your money moves in and out of your banking account over a period of time. A personal budget sheet typically spans a month because most bills are due monthly. Car payments, credit card payments, cell phone bills, and rent or mortgage payments are all due monthly. Look at how much money you make during a month and compare that to how much you have in expenses that month.

Once you know how much money you have, you can start spending it on the things you want to spend it on without stressing over it. You no longer have to worry about running out of money before you need to pay your rent or car payment. A budget will let you enjoy your life and your money. Once you are able to explain this to your student, and demonstrate a few examples in your life how a lack of a budget has hurt or having one has helped, they will be on their way to understanding the value of a budget.

Budgeting is a process, but not a complicated one. In fact it is quite easy. Sticking to the budget is the difficult part because it does not simply involve numbers. It involves taking action and using self-discipline. Don't worry about that part for now. Once your student understands the big picture, the behavior part will take care of itself.

The College Budget

One of the biggest mistakes students make is spending their student loan disbursements within the first few weeks after receiving them. It is difficult for anyone to be cautious when they have $3,000 in a checking account or on a prepaid student debit card, such as Higher One. Suddenly, $10 to dine out, $4 for a coffee or energy drink, and $25 for two movie tickets all seem like a drop in the bucket. So how can your student avoid the temptation of spending all of his or her money too fast? By budgeting.

At the beginning of each semester help your student determine how much money they have coming in from financial aid and other one-time sources. Add in any amounts they will receive from you, grandparents, family members, and anyone else that gives them money. Then subtract out any one-time expenses such as tuition, books, supplies, and travel. Also, don't forget about things like dues for student organizations, a planned road trip, or a flight back home. Deduct these expenses first.

Now divide the remaining amount by the number of months until their next financial aid disbursement and put this as the amount of spending money they have each month until the beginning of the next semester or their next disbursement.

Let's say that they receive $2,500 in financial aid loans and $500 from their uncle at the beginning of the semester. Instead of seeing $3,000 in their account, you want them to determine how long it will be until their next financial aid disbursement and help them make their money last for that length of time. After subtracting out books, travel, and other expenses, they have $1,200 left. This still may sound like a lot of money to a college student. But they have to make that $1,200 last six months. Now it's not so much money. From the original $3,000 at the beginning of the semester your student only has $200 per month to last them until the next semester. It becomes more difficult for them to waste money when they see they have only $200 per month rather than $3,000 per semester. By focusing on the smallest number rather than the largest they can begin to control their spending.

Let's work through completing the following college budget.

MY COLLEGE BUDGET		EXAMPLE
Financial aid disbursements	$ _____	2,500
+ Other one-time money	$ _____	500
= Total Starting Money	$ _____	3,000
Books & supplies	- _____	400
Parking	- _____	100
Membership dues	- _____	400
Travel / break	- _____	600
Moving expenses	- _____	200
Other one-time expenses	- _____	100
= Total Spending Money	$ _____	1,200
Divide by # of months money must last (usually 5 or 6)	/ _____	6
Put this amount as their Spending money into each of the columns on the next chart:	_____	200

	Month 1	M 2	M 3	M 4	M 5	M 6
Spending Money	$	$	$	$	$	$
Other Income	+	+	+	+	+	+
Total Monthly Spending	=$	=$	=$	=$	=$	=$
Rent	-	-	-	-	-	-
Utilities	-	-	-	-	-	-
Car Payment	-	-	-	-	-	-
Insurance	-	-	-	-	-	-
Travel/ Gas	-	-	-	-	-	-
Other Expenses	-	-	-	-	-	-
Food	-	-	-	-	-	-
Leftover for Going Out	=$	=$	=$	=$	=$	=$

Next, add in any monthly sources of income. This would include money they expect to earn from their part-time job, work-study, or any other income sources. Now they know how much they have available to cover their monthly bills. Finally, subtract out their monthly expenses such as rent, utilities, car payments, etc.

That's it! Now they know how much is left over that they can spend on other things, like dining out. It is very simple and helps remove the stress from them and you of not knowing if they can cover all their bills and expenses toward the end of the semester. As long as they stay within that amount, they can relax.

You want their budget sheet to be simple while still being useful. Everyone should customize their budget sheet so that it makes the most sense for them. Maybe clothes and shoes should be separated. The example budget sheet is a great start, but as they track their money they may find their budget sheet needs constant modification as their situation changes from semester to semester.

In the beginning it is all about awareness of where the money is coming from, where it is going, and how long it can last. As your student reviews and updates his or her budget each month they will become more aware of where their money goes. After a semester or so they will be so attuned to where they spend their money that they can focus on what is really important: how to change their spending habits to increase their surpluses and reduce their shortages.

Surpluses and Shortages

The great news is that a surplus means your student can afford to pay for college and still have some money left over to use on their greatest priorities. Their budget allows them to see areas where they can cut spending and allocate more the following semester. That is why budgeting when properly done and understood is so much fun. If your student does have a surplus they should consider the source of the refund. If they have so much money left over that they do not need to work, but most of that money is coming from student loans that have to be repaid, it may make sense to return the excess loan amount and spend less, or get a part-time job if possible. A surplus that comes from borrowed money is not really a surplus at all.

If your student's budget statement indicates a shortage, then it's time to make some adjustments. Regular monthly shortages mean they will either borrow more money or they will need to pick up a part-time job to cover the shortfall. Some additional debt may be manageable but too much additional debt could be disastrous to their future ability to afford to live on their own. Almost every student can handle working 10-15 hours per week. In fact, studies indicate anything less than 20 hours per week has no negative impact on a student's academics.[xiv] Working more than 20 hours would likely be detrimental to their academic career. At least now you and your student can sit down and discuss what options are best.

Repeat

The final step of the college budgeting process is to repeat. It is especially important to look at each semester differently as there may be new or different expenses each semester. Perhaps your student's goals will change. Maybe they will switch majors late into their college career and need an extra semester. Maybe their job situation will change or they can pick up more hours or take additional classes during the summer. The key is to help your student stay in control of his or her money. They will have more choices and options along with less stress and worry.

Having a successful budget while in college will allow your student to manage his or her spending, avoid unnecessary financial stress, and graduate without excessive debt. Now that your student understands how to manage his or her money, their next step is to decide what financial institutions or services they should utilize to make their lives easier, but with the least amount of costs and fees.

Chapter 8
The Cash Box:
Banking at College

Knowing the best ways to pay for college and how to manage those dollars is an excellent start to a bright future. Now the question becomes, "what are the best tools?" If your student is working, receives a large financial aid disbursement, or has money from summer employment, they will need to keep their money somewhere. In fact, his or her college may decide to provide the reimbursement on a pre-loaded debit card. How can you help your student avoid the many pitfalls when it comes to spending, banking, and paying fees?

The Best Ways to "Bank" Your Money

Many parents and students choose credit unions because they tend to be less expensive, pay higher interest rates on deposits, and charge lower interest rates on loans. They usually exist for people with a common interest, such as working for the same company, or living in the same community. Since credit unions are owned by their members, their rates are more favorable. Others choose banks because they tend to offer a broader range of services, as well as more locations and automated teller machines (ATMs). The choice is yours and your student's. Your student is the consumer. It's your student's money, which makes them the boss. Your student should shop wisely, compare, and then decide which one is right for his or her current situation. Below is a handy chart that compares banks and credit unions.

Banks and Credit Unions

Banks

- More fees, such as teller fees, etc.
- Higher fees for bounced checks, ATMs
- More branches available
- More savings programs
- More loan programs
- Higher minimum balances
- More ATMs available
- Low interest rates on savings
- Very structured, more procedures/rules
- Higher interest rates on loans

Credit Unions

- Fewer fees
- Lower fees
- Usually only one location
- Fewer savings programs
- Fewer loan programs
- Low or no minimum balance
- Few ATMs available
- Higher interest rates on savings
- Loose structure, fewer procedures/rules
- Lower interest rates on loans

Checking Accounts

For your student to decide best where to deposit his or her financial aid disbursements, paychecks, or money from home, they need to know a little about checking accounts. Since most checking accounts operate pretty much the same, the focus should be on paying as little as possible in fees and charges.

Most credit unions and many banks offer free checking, especially if your student uses direct deposit. Being charged for a checking account is like having a wallet that charges your student every time they open it. There are so many choices that offer minimal or zero fees there is no excuse for using a bank that places a charge on a checking account. There are almost always better alternatives.

Here are some tips on avoiding checking fees.

- Direct Deposit: Many banks waive account fees if your student's paycheck is direct deposited into their account.
- Average Daily Balance: Some banks charge a fee if your student's account balance falls below a certain amount any time during the month. Look for a bank that bases its fees on the average daily balance method. As long as the balance averages more than the minimum requirement your student will not pay a fee.
- Basic Checking: Some banks offer a basic checking account that pays no interest but requires no minimum balance. They may limit the number of checks your student can write and the number of ATM withdrawals they can make. This won't work if your student frequently uses the ATM. Many banks also offer student checking accounts with no fees.
- Avoid ATM Fees: Some banks charge each time your student uses their ATM. If your student is a frequent user of ATMs and his or her bank charges to use their ATM, your student should find a bank that does not. What about an out-of-network ATM? How much do they charge per transaction? Check to see if there are only a limited number of free transactions per month. In addition, some banks charge a fee to use a debit card. That's right; your student could pay for the privilege of spending his or her own money at the grocery store. Always look at the fine print. If your student is charged to use their debit card then they should find another bank.

Checks

While paper checks seem to be going the way of the dinosaur they still serve their purpose on some occasions. To make life easier, your student should use carbon checks so they keep record of who they paid, how much, and when. While they can view a scanned picture of the check online at most banks; that only works once the checks are cashed. What happens if they write a check and the recipient doesn't cash it for several months? They never have to wonder "Did I remember to pay that bill by check?" or "What did I buy with check number 1701?" Carbon copy checks may be a bit more expensive but they are not going to write very many anyway.

Save some money by avoiding fancy or custom checks. Save even more money by purchasing checks from a reputable check printing company rather than the bank. Like any other purchase, it pays to shop around. Remind your student to never sign a blank check! Anyone could fill in any dollar amount and cash it.

Bounced Checks

It is imperative that your student avoid bouncing a check. A bounced check (not having enough money in the account to cover the check) is not only illegal, but it is also costly. Almost all banks and merchants charge a fee, usually around $35 per bounced check. That means your student's bank can charge $35 for bouncing a check, and the merchant (store) where they tried to pay with that check can also charge $35 for writing the bad check to them. One bounced check could cost your student $70 or more plus a lot of embarrassment. Of course, one bounced check will not destroy them financially, but making a habit of it will. If your student routinely bounces checks then they really should keep a balanced checkbook.

It's easy for your student to balance his or her checking account. There are many small paper registers that allow them to track when they write a check or make an ATM withdrawal, and when they make a deposit. Once a month they should review their statement and subtract out any other charges. The goal is for them to avoid running out of money before the end of the month.

If that doesn't sound like something your student would stick with then they should choose a bank or credit union that has their account details easily available online. They can browse their account every few days to see which online payments have cleared and which have not. Since they use the carbon checks they can also see if there are any checks yet to clear. Plus, this is the easiest way to keep track of their ATM or bankcard withdrawals. Most banks post their transactions in real-time, although some still have a one or two-day delay. Students should keep this in mind when choosing a bank and when monitoring their account online.

Overdraft Protection

One option to protect your student from having payments rejected or bouncing checks is to use overdraft protection. There are two types. The first links their savings account with their checking account so if they spend more than is in their checking account the bank transfers money from their savings account to cover the charges. This only works if they have enough money in their savings account. Of course, most banks charge a small fee for each transfer.

Another type of overdraft protection banks offer is to automatically deposit a set amount into their checking account, such as $500, when they spend more than is in the account. This is a loan from the bank. It works well if they do not have enough in savings. However, the bank charges interest on this loan and it can be costly over time. The fees are usually higher and the interest rates may vary. Yet it is still less expensive than having a payment rejected due to lack of funds.

Automatic Withdrawals

Automatic withdrawals or Electronic Funds Transfers (EFT) are when a company automatically deducts payments from a checking account. For instance, your student's car insurance or rent may be withdrawn electronically every month. Your student must account for these transactions on their budget statement each month.

Cashing a Check

When your student deposits or cashes a check, banks are allowed to hold the funds for a certain number of days. The bank gets to make sure the person who wrote the check has enough money in their account. The money is usually available the next day, but in certain instances the money may not be available for up to five days. This can be especially true for college students depositing out of state checks. Your student should be mindful of this when they make a deposit and plan to spend that money immediately. They should log in online to see if the bank has credited the money to their account before they try to spend any recent deposits. Your student can check with his or her bank or credit union about their specific check holding policies.

Automated Teller Machines (ATMs)

Most banks do not charge their own customers to use their ATM machines. However, many banks charge a $2 - $4 fee to use their ATM if your student is not their customer. In addition, your student's own bank may charge them another $2 - $4 because they used another bank's ATM. They could end up paying as much as $8 just to get to their own money! No wonder there are so many ATMs available.

Your student should keep his or her ATM receipt. Otherwise, it's much harder for them to keep tabs on their account balance. In addition, while most machines only print the last few digits of the account, and a few digits may seem unimportant, the less other people know about their bank accounts the better.

Debit Cards

Does your student know what a debit card is? It uses the same networks as credit cards; hence the VISA™ or MasterCard™ logo on most of them. Your student swipes them through the same machine at the store as a credit card. Unlike a credit card, when they use their debit card, they are spending their own money that they already have in their account. Your student has to first deposit money into his or her account in order to use their debit card.

Normally a debit card is linked to a checking account, but it can be linked to a savings account or money market account as well. It can also be linked to other accounts such as a flexible spending account for health insurance or a meal plan at college. In fact, many colleges actually load financial aid disbursements onto debit cards. The important distinction is that your student is not borrowing money when using a debit card. They are actually using their money. Of course, if the money they are spending is from their financial aid disbursement, and if that money is from student loans, then they are still spending borrowed money. They are just not borrowing additional money. The debit card simply functions as a tool to give them access to their student loan dollars.

How to Use a Debit Card

Yes, there is an entire section on using a debit card. Who knew it was complicated? But not knowing the details of how a debit card works can cost your student a lot of money in fees over the long run. Let's dive in.

When your student makes a purchase at the store they normally have the option of selecting credit or debit. Choosing debit requires them to enter their personal identification number or PIN. Choosing credit means they are required to sign a receipt. Why is this important? Because of the way debit cards and credit cards work, some banks charge a small fee each time your student uses their debit card as a debit card (where they key in their PIN). Selecting credit avoids the small fee. This does not mean that your student is borrowing money with their debit card the way credit cards work. The difference is that they did not pay the extra fee. Either way the money comes directly from their account.

One of the advantages of a debit card is they can get additional cash back when they make a purchase at the grocery or convenience store. They can choose the debit option if they want extra cash, but they don't want to let the fees creep up on them. Many banks charge a small fee to cover any costs associated with providing this service. Typically these fees are listed as POS or "point of sale" fees on a bank statement.

If your student has a tight budget, as most students do, they should watch out for a little-known trap. Some merchants put a block on their account when they buy gas. When they swipe their debit card, the gas station does not know how much gas they need so they "block" $50-$75 or even $100 of their account just to make sure there is enough to pay for the gas. Usually within two days the portion of the $75 that they did not use will be released and is available to them again. This is when it becomes important. Say they have $100 in their account and they only get $50 in gas. They expect $50 to still be available. But if they try to buy something for $50 their card is declined because they have access to only $25 thanks to the $75 block. As the card industry technology improves, the large block on the card is becoming less common but it still happens.

College Debit Cards

Finally, watch out for college debit cards. Many card companies, and even banks, partner with a college to offer a debit card specific to that college. Some colleges even turn your student's ID card into a debit card. Schools use these cards to disburse student loans, scholarships, grants, and other financial aid to students. They are debit cards with the balance left over after tuition, room, and board are all paid. They operate just like any other debit card from a bank, but with many more hidden fees. While these fees can take a significant bite out of your student's financial aid, it's all legal. That is because it is a debit card only and not a credit card, so it does not fall under the protection of the Credit Card Act of 2009.

Why would a college partner with a card company? It allows the college to reduce its costs to administer financial aid and other money transactions between the college and your student. The good news is that these cards do not charge interest. The disadvantage is that the cards are all fee based instead. That means it's your student that pays all the fees.

For example, most college debit cards charge a small fee every time your student swipes the card to buy books, groceries, gas, or anything else. Overdrawn or non-sufficient funds charges are higher than most banks and credit unions, and they charge a $25 fee or more to transfer their balance off the card to their regular account. They even charge an inactivity fee, sometimes as much as $19 per month, if your student does not use the card within a certain period of time.

It is easy for your student to avoid many of these fees by opening an account at a bank or credit union with more favorable terms and transferring the balance to their account. Or they can request that the school issue a check and they can deposit the money for themselves. They should be careful to read the fine print as there is usually a fee to transfer large amounts off the card to their account. The disadvantage of having the school send a check directly to them is that it takes an additional week or two to receive their financial aid money.

Bottom line is that banks and credit unions are just like any other purchase. Ultimately, your student is the customer. That makes your student always right when it comes to choosing the program and institution that is right for him or her. More important, it is his or her money. Your student is the boss. Many banks and credit unions work to help your student with what they believe is in their best interest, but they do so with only the products and services they have to offer. Another bank may offer a better program but your student is expected to figure that out on his or her own. Your student should comparison shop for a bank just like they would any other purchase.

Credit Cards

Many experts will tell your student to avoid credit cards at all cost. Others say your student should definitely have credit cards for a whole host of different reasons. It's difficult to know whose advice to follow. Credit cards can be a wonderful convenience. However, their abuse leads to wrecking more people's finances, especially students', than any other single thing they do. The key to credit cards is to understand how they work, what purpose they should serve, and when your student should and should not use them.

Credit cards are not bad by themselves. They are simply a tool. Really they are more like a power tool in some regards. In a shop class you are not allowed to use the power tools until you receive the proper training and are supplied with the proper safety equipment. Likewise, you are not allowed to drive a car without first receiving training and being issued a license. Yet, most people can easily get a credit card without receiving any warnings, safety training, or basic instructions. In fact, the credit card industry employs some of the most predatory lending practices of any type of lender or creditor from which a person can borrow money.

Not all is lost. The 2009 Credit Card Accountability, Responsibility, and Disclosure Act (the Credit CARD Act) changed some of the rules of the credit card industry in an attempt to protect consumers. Credit card companies can no longer solicit your student on college campuses and it is more difficult for your student to open a credit card before the age of 21. Students now must prove they have the income necessary to make the payments on the credit card or they must get a cosigner. Sadly, before this law was enacted, 76% of undergraduates had credit cards with an average balance of $2,200.[xv] Other changes included the elimination of questionable practices such as universal default and two-cycle billing. The law requires credit card bills to be sent at least 21 days before the payment is due, requires payments to be credited up to 5 p.m. on the due date, and adds multiple restrictions on fees and rates.[xvi]

The changes were designed to provide greater consumer protection. The biggest gap in the law was that interest rates were not capped. Credit card companies are still free to charge whatever rate they want, particularly for adjustable rate cards. Card companies do have to notify card holders at least 45 days before a rate changes.

All of these practices were used by credit card companies in the past to increase their revenues. They employ attorneys, smart finance professors, and behavioral scientists to find consumer behaviors that occur frequently and could be used to make money. Now that the laws have changed, it is even more important that you and your student are aware of what practices credit card companies will develop next. It's a sure bet they will be looking for new ways to earn more profits, such as new fees, increased rates, or other approaches that have not yet been discovered.

Advantages of Credit Cards

Even with all the dangers that come with using credit cards there are several advantages that make having a credit card worth considering. The biggest advantage is that they simply provide a huge convenience. Your student does not need to carry cash to make purchases with credit cards. In addition, a credit card allows them to buy now and pay later. Bookkeeping is also much easier because they (or you) can use their monthly credit card statement to identify where they spend their money.

Another big advantage of credit cards is that they offer protection. Credit cards provide more protection from fraud and poor business practices than cash. Using cash may make it more difficult to return a product or dispute a service with a company that did not deliver what was promised. Upon the cardholder's request the credit card company will stop the payment to a store or vendor so your student will not be charged or defrauded. Credit cards also offer much more protection for online purchases and limit the amount of money you or your student can lose if someone steals their card or their card number. They cannot get all these same protections with a wallet full of cash.

Disadvantages of Credit Cards

There are several disadvantages to credit cards as well. The biggest disadvantage is they are simply more convenient. Yes, the key advantage of credit cards is also their key disadvantage. Due to their convenience, your student can obligate their future income too easily. Their ability to buy now and pay later often means that they buy too much now and have too much to pay later. Using credit cards irresponsibly results in wasted money in high interest rates and other hidden costs.

The ease of credit provided by credit cards makes it very easy to overspend. People tend to buy items on the spot that they would otherwise take time to think about and consider. They don't take time to consult their budget or to make sure a purchase is aligned with their financial goals. Credit cards allow your student to sidestep their own self-discipline. With a credit card in hand they can make that purchase without giving themselves time to really think about it.

The real danger when using credit cards is the complexity of the rules. When your student signs a credit card application, they sign a contract. If the credit card company gives them one of their credit cards, your student agrees to play by the card company's rules. For example, because interest rates are not capped your student may end up paying exorbitant interest rates. Some are well over 20%, particularly on department store cards. If they make one payment 60 days late or more, then their rate could easily go above 30%. Late payment fees and over the limit fees easily reach as high as $25 or $35 if it is not their first offense (the fees were $39 before the recent Credit CARD Act).[xvii]

In addition, most credit card companies offer a grace period, a few days between the time your student makes a purchase and the time when the credit card begins charging interest. If your student pays the entire balance during the grace period then they pay no interest. However, if they carry a balance on the credit card then the grace period disappears. Your student begins paying interest expense the moment they buy something, even before they have had a chance to pay it off.

The credit card industry is extremely competitive. In order to lure your student into using a credit card, many companies offer zero percent interest for a short time such as the first six months. All your student has to do is transfer their balance from their current card to the new card. However, most cards charge a 4% "transfer" fee. If your student transfers a $1,000 balance from their old card to the new card they will now owe $1,040 ($1,000 original balance plus the $40 transfer fee). They get 0% interest for six months, but had to pay 4% to transfer the amount. After the six-month introductory rate ends, the rate adjusts to whatever the standard rate is for that card. The 4% transfer fee is nothing more than an 8% annualized interest rate disguised as a 4% six-month fee.[xviii] It's really not much of a deal at all.

Shop Around

Just like any other purchase your student makes, they should shop around for a credit card that best meets their needs. Cards come in all varieties with different interest rates, rules, annual fees, reward points, and so forth. They can shop around using sites such as www.CardWeb.com™.[xix] They can find the credit card that is best suited for them. They can search for balance transfer offers, reward points, low interest rates, and more. CardWeb™ even has a category specifically for students. Keep in mind that your student is the customer. He or she is doing the card company a favor by choosing their card, not the other way around.

Your student should read the offer (which is the contract) to determine if there are restrictions or fees they do not like. Every credit card application has a box (called the Schumer box) that summarizes most of the key points of the contract, including the annual fee, the interest rate, the grace period, and other fees.[xx]

Your Student is the Boss

Two things bear repeating. Your student is the customer; that makes them the boss over the card company. And the credit card industry is very competitive. That gives your student a lot of power. If your student does not like the way their credit card company is treating them; they should switch. The card companies know it is very easy for your student to switch to one of their competitors. That makes them willing to do what is necessary to keep your student as a customer.

It's easy for your student to call their current credit card company and negotiate better terms. They can call them at any time and ask for a better rate. Simply state that they have a better offer from another company, they have been a loyal customer, and they want their current card company to match the better offer. Many times they will get a lower rate. Even if the card company does not say "yes" there was no cost to ask.

If your student is late on a payment, they should call the company and ask to have the late fee waived. Your student should let them know that they regularly pay their bills on time and that this was an unusual case. In addition, they should let the card company know they expect no increase in their interest rate. If the card company is reluctant to agree, your student should take their business elsewhere. Remember, your student is the customer. They are the boss of the credit card company. There are a lot of other companies out there that really want their business. Of course, this works only if your student pays their bills on time. If your student makes a habit of late payments they will end up paying a lot of money in late fees, see their interest rate rise, damage their credit score, and the credit card company will be very unlikely to work with them. If they are in good standing, they have a much better chance of getting better terms from the credit card company than if they abuse or misuse their credit.

Your student needs to make their payments on time. They can use automatic direct draft or online bill pay from their bank. They will need to monitor their minimum payment as it will change each month as their credit card balance changes. They should keep their e-mail confirmation or print the confirmation page for their files as verification they made their payment. In the event that a credit card company tries to argue that they did not pay on time, they will have proof. If the card company tries to do anything you or your student thinks is unethical or illegal, first try to resolve the issue with the credit card company. If you or your student are not able to resolve the issue directly with the credit card issuer, then you can make a complaint to the office of the attorney general for your state. The attorney general's contact information can be found at www.naag.org.[xxi]

Bottom Line

A credit card is a huge convenience, but makes it extremely easy for your student to blow his or her finances right out of the water. What can they do? Recognize that a credit card is nothing more than a tool (a really powerful tool). It's just one part of a comprehensive strategy for your student to manage his or her finances while they are on the road to accomplishing their financial goals. A credit card simply provides your student an added level of convenience. It is not an excuse for them to bypass their budget, ignore their goals, or skirt their own financial self-control.

Almost There

At this point you have been able to help your student see the big picture, avoid the common pitfalls, succeed in college, pay for college the right way, and manage his or her money. Your student is well on his or her way to becoming a successful college graduate who will NOT be moving home after graduation. As your student heads into the final semester of his or her senior year, the number one thing that will keep your kid from moving back home after graduation is landing a good job. After all, that was the big picture. That was why they (and you) went through this whole college process in the first place.

Chapter 9
Time to Pack up:
The Keys to Getting a Job

Although it will take some time for your student to answer the three "W"s, improve himself or herself, position himself or herself, complete an internship, and get good grades, eventually they will reach their last semester in college. That is when they need to begin to market themselves. It will not be enough to just acquire a great education, skills, and experiences, but they must convince an employer that they have all of these. It will take a lot of hard work that includes a good resume and cover letter, lots of practice interviews, research, and follow-up. In fact, the job of getting a job is a job!

The Resume

The purpose of your student's resume is not to get them a job, but to get them an interview. Because their resume is their primary marketing tool, it must be perfect. There can be no mistakes or misspellings. Their first and only chance to impress a potential employer or hiring manager is through their resume. If they do not pay attention to details on something this important, it gives the impression that they will not pay attention to details in other areas of their work, so no company will want to hire them.

Their resume must say what they need it to say in just a page or two. They should go through many edits of their resume. Your student will need to study a resume writing guide or two. There are many very good resources available online, such as the Rockport Institute's website (www.rockportinstitute.com). Encourage your student to take a resume writing workshop from the career office at their college. They can ask their professors to review it. They (or you) can ask people they (or you) know who hire people to review it. Your student wants as much feedback as he or she can get in order to build the best possible resume.

Most students have never considered the hiring process from the hiring manager's perspective. The manager has a job opening posted in the newspaper and on the Web. Now they have 250 resumes to sort through to select three candidates to bring in for an interview. Keep in mind that they still have their other work to do. How in the world is that manager going to narrow a pile of 250 resumes down to just five or ten? They start looking for ways to eliminate candidates, such as any resume with a misspelled word or of unnecessary length. Applicants with a less than perfect resume are the first to go. Your student does not want to be eliminated from consideration because of a silly mistake on their resume.

Your student's resume is a critical document. Not only does it need to be right, it needs to be perfect. And the only right resume is the one that gets them an interview. Your student will be interviewing with a specific employer; therefore, the resume must be tailored to that employer. This means if your student is applying for different jobs, they will have a slightly different resume for each job application. Each resume emphasizes their strengths related to the requirements of each job. For example, if looking for a job in sales, then they need to emphasize their experience in sales or dealing one-on-one with other people. On the other hand, if applying for a graphic design position, they would emphasize their accomplishments in artistic and printing areas.

Once your student is ready to submit his or her resume, be sure they print the final version. For any electronic submission, they should make sure the file is clearly named so they will easily be able to attach the correct version. If they are submitting to an online posting, it is important to avoid all formatting other than simple text and indents. Bullets, lines, and other advanced formatting features do not always transmit well electronically. If submitting via e-mail, advise your student to make sure they attach the correct file and review any text within the body of their e-mail message for misspellings. Then they should double-check that they attached the correct file by opening the attachment. Their resume and e-mail must be perfect before they hit "send."

The Cover Letter

Although your student's resume is the tool that will help them get an interview, it is their cover letter that will get their resume read by the potential employer. If they just send a resume without a cover letter it may be ignored, set aside, or trashed. The cover letter is their first opportunity to introduce themselves to an employer. Without a cover letter their resume is just a list of classes, job tasks, and responsibilities. The cover letter brings it all together and allows your student to say, "I am a real person who you want to consider hiring so go ahead and look through my resume and then call me to set up an interview and learn more." They do not literally write that on their cover letter of course, but that is what their cover letter represents.

Just like their resume, their cover letter should be customized for each individual job for which they are applying. They will need to research each potential employer to learn enough about the company to sound very interested and knowledgeable. They want to start the letter by directing it to an actual person. They should use the contact information on the job application or find out who the hiring manager is. Even when applying through a human resources department it is a good idea for them to send a cover letter and resume to the person actually doing the hiring.

The cover letter should be brief, concise, and just three paragraphs long. The first paragraph should say who your student is and how they learned of the job opening. The next paragraph should explain why your student is the best person for the job. The final paragraph should tell the employer how to contact them. Keep in mind the people who will read the cover letter are very busy, and your student wants to illustrate they value their future employer's time. Nobody wants to read a page filled with small font text that is boring and not relevant. Your student wants to whet the employer's appetite so they want to review the resume.

Once your student has completed their resume and cover letter, it is time for them to start sticking stamps on envelopes and applying for jobs. Not only will they stick stamps, but they will also spend many hours completing online job applications. Regardless of the way they apply, what is important for them to remember is not to become discouraged. They will hear the word "No" many more times than they will hear the word "Yes." That is the nature of the game. They should keep in mind that it only takes one "Yes" to land an interview and one interview to get a job offer.

The Interview

Congratulations, your student made it through round one! The hiring manager read their cover letter and resume and is interested enough to schedule an interview. The first thing they need to do is get a contact number from the interviewer or the human resources department in case they need to contact them. Now the real work begins. There is much more to an interview than just showing up and answering some basic questions. Your student has to prepare.

Research

Preparing for the interview is like cramming for an exam. They need to find out as much as they can about the company. One of the worst things they can do is walk into the interview totally unprepared with little or no knowledge of the company. They should start with the basics and find out what the company does and how they make their money. Then, find out how the company did last year and what their goals and objectives are. Next, research how many employees the company has, in how many countries, who their competitors are, and what the outlook is for their industry.

Your student should find out if the company has received any awards recently or if they have received any bad press. They can listen to the chairman's address to the board of directors to determine the current priorities and direction of the company. They should Google the company to track down the most recent annual report, which contains more information than just sales figures. They should also review the company website for important and recent news. The key is for your student to show the interview committee that they actually have an interest in the company and not just in the job.

This is where your student's college career plan really pays off. Imagine how much they will know about a company if it's a company they identified as one they wanted to work for back when they were a sophomore and interned with when they were a junior.

Practice

It has been said many times that practice makes perfect. Although perfection may be a standard that is difficult to achieve, practice does certainly lead to improvement. The only way for your student to get better at interviews is to practice. If they don't want their practice to be at the first real interview where mistakes can blow their chances at getting a job, then they need to practice mock interviews with other people such as friends and family. Feel free to offer to interview your student, even if it is over the phone. Better yet they should use their college's career services office's interview workshops and practice interviews.

To get the most out of practice interviews, your student must be willing to accept criticism and work on improving their interview skills. The more they practice, the more confident and polished they will become. A confident person is more likely to get selected than a timid one. Your student does not want to go in and act like they own the world, but they do want to act and look like they belong.

The Elevator Speech

It is important for your student to have an elevator speech. This is a 20-30 second summary of who they are and what they are looking to do. The idea is that if they get on an elevator and the hiring manager steps in, your student will be able to confidently look him or her in the eye and explain why they are the best candidate for a job with that company.

A good elevator speech would go something like, "Hello, my name is Pat Doe and I have a bachelor's degree in underwater basket weaving with internship experience at Underwater Hammocks, Inc. As an active member of the student chapter of Underwater Basket Weavers International I have successfully participated in many leadership roles, and I am now ready to take what I have learned and translate that into success at your company. I am looking forward to speaking with your hiring manager about job possibilities in your aquatics weaving department." Of course, your student has to make the speech his or her own but you get the idea. While it is doubtful your student will ever get on an elevator with the president of some company, there are many other times where that speech will be useful. Their elevator speech will be used at career fairs, networking events, and other occasions where they run into potential employers and other contacts.

Arrive Early

Now that your student has practiced interviewing several times and has researched the company, they can go into the interview with confidence. They should be sure to arrive at the interview early; otherwise they are adding stress to an already stressful situation. If they show up late for an interview, they are already done before they begin. With very few exceptions, such as a major traffic issue so severe it actually makes the news, they may not even get a chance to have the interview. In the event that they are running late due to unforeseen circumstances, it is time to dial that phone number they wrote down when they scheduled the interview. They should call and calmly explain the situation and ask if there is any way they can still be seen, or in extreme circumstances, they may have to ask if they can hold the interview over the phone because traffic is not moving, their airplane was delayed, etc. Remember, the employer does not know what is going on if your student does not tell them.

To avoid any last-minute surprises, it's a good idea for your student to drive to the place where the interview will be held at least one day in advance and at the same time as the interview. They should check for the amount of time it will take to arrive, where they can park, and even confirm the exact floor and office number within the building. Point out to your student that during rush hour in major cities it is not uncommon to spend 30 minutes or more traveling a total of three or four miles. The more prepared they are when they walk into the interview, the less stressed they will be.

Show Confidence

Now that your student has done all their preparations and arrived 30 to 60 minutes ahead of time, they can relax and review their research about the position and the company until it is time to go inside the building. Tell them to not drink coffee or other caffeinated drinks or anything that can spill and stain their clothes just before the interview. They should drink only water to keep their throat from getting dry. When it is time, they can just relax and be confident that they can do this. They are about to convince a handful of professionals that their company, as good as it already is, will be better when they have your student as one of their employees.

Since the first real introduction usually begins with a handshake, it becomes an important first impression. Your student should firmly shake the other person's hand when introduced. You don't want them breaking any knuckles, but they should also avoid a weak or limp handshake. A firm handshake indicates confidence. Because your student is relaxed, their palms will not be too sweaty either.

Remind them to always keep a smile on their face. They want to look enthusiastic, not scared or unsure of themselves. They should look the interviewer in the eye while being asked questions and when they are responding. Eye contact indicates confidence and sincerity.

Questions and Answers

Silence during an interview can trip up your student. They should be aware that once they answer a question during an interview, they need to be quiet and not say anything more. Silence is an interview tactic designed to get your student to reveal much more about themselves than they ever intended. They should answer questions succinctly, but completely. Then be quiet. For instance, after answering the question, "Why did you apply for this position?" with a simple explanation of their high regard for the company and how well it aligns with their background and goals, your student is done. The interviewer is satisfied with their answer. But if the interviewer lets a few seconds of silence go by, your student may be tempted to ramble on. They want to avoid, "I have already applied for many other jobs that actually are a better fit but because I have not heard back from any of them I figured even though sales is not really my main focus I could give it a try because it is better than nothing." At that point your student can just use the rest of the interview as practice for their next one because they just lost this job opportunity.

Your student will also be asked if they have any questions for the interviewer. Here, they can rely on their research so they can ask intelligent questions of their own. Good questions are ones that indicate to the interviewer that your student did his or her homework, they understand the job and the company, and they are generally interested in this job. Remind your student to not ask about salary, vacations, and other perks. That indicates to the employer that salary and time off are more important to your student than the job. Salary and benefits will come in due time, after the offer has been extended. If they are not interested in offering your student the position, then those things do not matter anyway.

Collect Business Cards

Your student should be sure to collect a business card from each interviewer or at least get their name and title. At the very least, they need to get the correct spelling and title of each interviewer from the receptionist or from the person who escorts them to the interview. If all else fails, they can research the company directory on their website. This will be important a couple of days after the interview.

After the Interview

So why did your student have to collect the correct spelling of everyone's name and title? They are now going to write a personalized thank-you note to each individual that interviewed them. The whole purpose of the thank-you note is to keep their name in front of the hiring committee or manager. The best time to send their thank-you letter is within 24 to 48 hours after the interview. If they are sending a thank-you via e-mail they should be sure to include their name in the subject line. The thank-you should hit the high notes of the interview focusing on specific questions or topics that resonated with each interviewer. This way each person receives their own individual thank-you, which is critical in the event they share with each other.

Remember, your student's goal is to get their name back on the top of the pile by making each interviewer feel special. They want to keep their note brief and concise, so they should only hit one or two high points. They should be sure to use proper grammar and spelling. They should read the e-mail or letter again and again and have someone else read it at least once. Once they are satisfied that it is perfect, they can send it. Then they can just sit back and wait for the job offers to come in.

Chapter 10
Non-Perishable: Student Loan Payments

While everyone would prefer not to owe any money for their college education, for most students the reality is they end up borrowing at least some money. The good news is that federal student loans are some of the friendliest loans they will ever have. There are many repayment options available for almost every situation. Every repayment option is designed to make sure your student can afford their payments. The key is to know what loans you and your student have and what the best options are. Ultimately, your student must manage their student loans or else their student loans will manage them.

Our discussion is going to get just a little bit technical. The rules and options are very complex, but it is important that you and your student understand them so they can make good decisions when it comes to their student loans. It is up to them to initiate the conversation with a financial aid counselor at their school before graduation if possible, or at any time before the loans are paid off.

Know What Is Owed

Before graduation, your student should ask the financial aid office to provide a list of all of his or her student loans that were processed through their office. Your student should monitor their loans each year while in college, but it is imperative that they know the total amount they owe before they graduate. If your student attended other colleges or universities, they will need to contact those financial aid offices as well. The goal is to collect as much information as possible about how much and from whom they borrowed money to attend college. No one wants to miss a payment only because they did not know it existed.

The next step is to look at the National Student Loan Data System (NSLDS) at www.nslds.ed.gov. The NSLDS is the U.S. Department of Education's central database for federal student loans. All of your student's federal student loans along with all their details will be listed in this database. For each federal loan there will be the type of loan, the lender, the loan servicer, the loan amount, the date the loan originated and was disbursed, if the loan was cancelled, the outstanding principal, and any outstanding interest on the loan. Keep in mind that private student loans will **_not_** be listed in the NSLDS, which is why your student should get a list of all loans from their financial aid office.

Next, your student should add up the total disbursements according to their financial aid office and make sure it matches what they find in the NSLDS. If it appears they borrowed more than what the NSLDS indicates, then they probably have some private student loans as well. If it appears the other way around, then they should contact the Department of Education to verify their loan information.

Now your student should make a list of who they owe, how much they owe, what the interest rates are, what the monthly payments are, when their payments are due, and the contact information of their loan servicer. They should keep the list readily accessible and not packed away in a box with their college souvenirs. At some point they are going to need it. There is a good chance that over the life of your student's loans something will go wrong.

At some point your student will need to talk to someone about his or her loans. This person is called a servicer. The servicer is a person that is hired by the lender to oversee the repayment process, including collection of their loan payment. Rarely, if at all, will your student ever talk to the people that actually loaned them the money.

Everyone talks about a grace period on student loans, but there is some confusion on this topic. Federal student loans grant a six-month (Stafford loans) or nine-month (Perkins loans) period after your student leaves school before they need to begin making their loan payments. This does not mean they have six or nine months before they have to contact their loan servicer or start making arrangements to pay back their loans. If a problem is apparent, such as no job or low income, the loan servicer should be contacted immediately. In addition, most private lenders offer no such grace period. It is important that your student meet with his or her financial aid counselor before they graduate to determine exactly what they owe and what the best repayment options are for them. If your student is unable to make his or her payments when the time comes, it is up to them to contact the servicer; not the other way around. If they wait until the servicer contacts them, they will have far fewer options available.

Choose a Repayment Plan

Federal student loans are some of the friendliest loans ever. Your student gets to choose the repayment plan that fits his or her particular situation best. There are several options, but if your student does not make a choice, he or she is automatically placed in the standard payment option. So what are the payment options?

Standard Payments

The standard repayment plan is for 10 years. Your student makes 120 equal monthly payments at a fixed interest rate. At the end of the 10 years the loan is paid off.

Graduated Payments

The graduated payment plan begins with smaller payments than the standard repayment plan, but increases the monthly payment every few years. By the end of the loan period, the payment is larger than what the standard monthly payment would have been. This plan works well for anyone who begins their career in a low-paying job, but expects to quickly move up the income ladder. Typically the loan period is 10 years. But your student should not select the graduated payment plan just to get the lower initial payments. The overall loan cost will be higher under this option than under the standard option, plus the monthly payments continue to get higher throughout the repayment plan.

Extended Payments

The extended repayment plan has a fixed monthly payment (it does not change) but the loan can last up to 25 years. Your student will have smaller monthly payments but the payments last much longer and your student pays more in interest. This plan is available only if your student has more than $30,000 in federal student loans. There is also a graduated extended payment option under this plan where the monthly payment starts out smaller and increases every few years. Be advised that this option will almost double the amount that your student ends up paying.

Payments Based on Income

Three payment plans will consider your student's income when determining the monthly payment amount. The income-sensitive repayment option bases the monthly payment amount on his or her annual income only. The income-contingent and income-based repayment plans consider his or her annual income, family size, and the state where he or she lives to determine the maximum amount your student can afford to pay each month. An advantage of the income-contingent and income-based plans is that any remaining portion of the loan at the end of the repayment period may be forgiven (your student will not owe any more money even if the loan is not totally paid off), but this is not guaranteed.

The disadvantage to the income-contingent and income-based plans is that the loan could end up lasting much longer than 10 years. In fact, it could be stretched out as long as 25 years, which means your student pays interest over a much longer period. The longer they make payments, the more they end up paying in interest. Plus they are required to reapply for this option every year and submit documentation to verify their income.

The best source for information on these options is in the repayment plans section at www.studentaid.ed.gov.

Comparing the Repayment Options

Confused? Let's take a look at an example. If your student were to graduate with a $35,000 federal student loan and an interest rate of 6.80%, the monthly payment amounts and the total amount he or she pay can vary a lot based on the payment option. Remember that in each case your student borrowed $35,000. Pay particular attention to the total amount paid column.

Your student should choose the repayment option that is the most practical for him or her and not just the one that has the smallest monthly payment. If you look only at the monthly payment amount, the extended payment plan is much better than the standard plan. However, your student is in debt for 25 years and pays almost $79,000 for that $35,000 loan. If your student is 22 years old when he or she graduates, they would be 47 years old when they finally pay off the school loan. At least with the standard plan your student is only 32 years old when the loan is paid off, not to mention that they paid less in interest and kept more money in their pocket.

Sample Student Loan Repayment Options[xxii]

	Monthly Payment	Interest Paid	Total Amount Paid	Years in Debt
Standard Repayment				
All Payments	$403	$13,334	$48,334	10
Extended Fixed Repayment				
All Payments	$243	$37,879	$72,879	25
Extended Graduated Repayment				
First Payment	$198	$43,939	$78,939	25
Final Payment	$347			
Graduated Repayment				
First Payment	$277	$15,944	$50,944	10
Final Payment	$604			
Income-Based Repayment[xxiii]				
First Payment	$172	$37,135	$72,759	21
Final Payment	$403			

Change the Plan

Once your student chooses a repayment plan they are not locked into that plan for life. They can switch from one repayment plan to another at least once a year. They can also pay off their student loans early in any amount at any time with no penalty.

Forgiveness

Although you or your student may hear or read something about student loans being forgiven, it is unlikely that they will meet the qualifications or receive any real benefit. In most cases, by the time they get to the point that they qualify for loan forgiveness their loan should have been paid off long ago. A lot more information about this option is available at www.studentaid.ed.gov in the 'Repaying Your Loans' section.

Consolidation

Consolidation simply means your student can combine all of his or her different loans into one big loan. Instead of having multiple loan payments to different servicers, they can consolidate their federal student loans so they have one payment. However, consolidation loans do not have a grace period. If your student consolidates his or her loans during the six-month grace period after they graduate or leave college, the first payment begins 60 days after the consolidation takes place. If they want or need to take advantage of the six-month grace period they can sign up for consolidation and schedule the consolidation to take place at the end of their grace period. Or they can wait until the last month of the grace period before consolidating.

Even though the different federal student loans may have different interest rates, consolidation loans have a single fixed rate. The government will use a weighted average interest rate, which basically means there is no interest rate advantage or disadvantage to consolidation except they round up by one-eighth percent. The advantage of consolidation is that your student makes only one large student loan payment instead of several smaller payments.

So your student can consolidate all of his or her student loans to have just one single payment, right? Not so fast. Only federal student loans can be consolidated together. Your student cannot consolidate any private student loans with their federal student loans. Private student loans have to be repaid separately. The good news is that they may be able to consolidate all their private student loans together as well, so that they have just two consolidation loans (and just two payments).

Be careful! Although federal student loans have various protections, including no consolidation fees, you and your student have to look carefully at the fine print for any consolidation that either of you do with your private loans. Private lenders calculate their interest rate any way they choose, and they will have more requirements and penalties.

No Money, No Payments

Despite your student's best efforts he or she is unable to find a job, found a job that does not pay very well, or their employer said "we no longer need your services." What can they do if the bills keep coming but the paychecks stop?

Your student should be proactive and contact the servicer and explain their situation *before* the servicer contacts them. This is why they made a list of all their loans and contact information and kept them easily accessible. The servicer will explain the options to your student and help them select the one that is best for their particular situation.

Whatever happens, your student should not ignore the servicer if they receive calls or letters about their payments. It is your student's responsibility to stay in touch with the servicer. Student loans do not go away. In fact, they will come back with a vengeance with harsh penalties. Because there are so many ways to work with the servicer no matter what the situation, there is no reason to avoid them. Instead, your student should explain his or her situation and see what the servicer can do to help.

Deferment

A deferment is a period of time where the servicer will allow your student to stop making payments. Servicers will defer student loan payments for reenrolling in college at least half-time (including graduate school), unemployment, economic hardship, or military service. Deferment simply extends the amount of time it takes to pay off the student loan debt. If your student has an unsubsidized loan, the interest will be added to the balance when the deferment period ends, so they end up owing even more money.

Forbearance

If your student is not eligible for deferment but still cannot make the payments, they may be eligible for forbearance. Forbearance means either they temporarily make smaller payments or stop making payments altogether. The loan continues to charge interest, even if it is a subsidized loan, but they have less drain on their cash flow temporarily. In almost all cases, your student must contact the servicer to request forbearance. The forbearance period and payment amount are based on his or her particular circumstances and they should only use the amount of forbearance time that they truly need. While forbearance can be helpful, it should be used sparingly because it results in more interest paid and a longer repayment term.

There Are Consequences

Not paying or defaulting on student loans will negatively affect everything your student wants to do in life. It will hinder them from getting a good job, buying a car, or leasing an apartment. Most important, it is unnecessary with federal student loans. Regardless of your student's situation, there are loan repayment options available. It is your student's responsibility to put forth the effort and contact the servicer to explain his or her circumstances. There are payment options to help them avoid unnecessary interest charges, bad credit, and unnecessary financial stress, but it is up to your student to make sure they know the ones that best fit their particular situation.

The important thing is for your student to not bury his or her head in the sand and hope the issue will go away. Their university, the lender, the state government, and the federal government all will take steps to get them to pay. For starters, their lender will report the delinquent loan to the credit bureaus, which will destroy your student's credit. The negative information remains on their credit report for seven years. Any federal payments, such as a tax refund, can be withheld to pay off their loan. In addition, extra fees and interest charges are added because of their failure to pay. As if that is not enough, their wages may also be garnished. That means their paycheck can be reduced as their employer sends a portion of their paycheck to the student loan lender. The lesson here is that your student should do everything in his or her power to not default on their student loans, ever.

One final warning, you and your student should not assume that bankruptcy can be used to get rid of federal student loans. The current law makes it extremely difficult to do so. In many instances your student may not be able to wipe out private student loans either. Thus, bankruptcy will destroy his or her credit for many years, and they still have to make their student loan payments. Instead, it is always better if they work with the servicer to work out a different arrangement for their student loans. Keep in mind that nobody wants your student to default on a loan. Everyone involved wants to help find a solution so the lender gets their money back.

Private Student Loans

We spent the last portion of this chapter explaining all of the options for federal student loans. What about private student loans? Unfortunately, there simply are not many options available to you or your student if either of you have private student loans. While initial rates may have been low, most private student loans have variable interest rates. Unlike federal loan rates that remain constant, anyone with private student loans could see their rates, and consequently their payments, rise. For the most part, private student loans need to be treated the same as any other consumer debt. The biggest difference is that it is nearly impossible to have them discharged in bankruptcy.[xxiv]

Lenders of private student loans have little incentive to work with your student since they know he or she cannot declare bankruptcy to get rid of that debt. Private student loans do not come with the advantage of all the repayment options offered with federal student loans. In addition, you may have been required to cosign for these loans. This means the lender can come after you for repayment if your student defaults. The best approach for your student to repay private student loans if they are having difficulty is to contact the lender, explain the situation, and try to get the lender to work out a more manageable repayment plan. Unfortunately, you and your student are at the mercy of the lender.

While private student loans do not need to be avoided altogether, financial aid administrators and even private lenders agree they should be used sparingly to fill gaps in need only after all other forms of aid are exhausted.[xxv]

Chapter 11
Return to Sender:
What if They Move Home
Anyway?

You and your student did everything right while they were in college. And you were just getting used to your empty nest. Yet your student graduates and they're back. For any number of reasons -- a tight job market, low salaries for entry-level jobs, high rent, or even student loan debt -- your new graduate is knocking on the door with suitcases in hand. Despite your and your student's best efforts, there are many factors that can lead to the real possibility of a "boomerang kid."

Boomerang Kids

According to a recent Huffington Post article, "85% of the class of 2011 will be forced to move back home." That is up from 69% in 2006. Over half of that group expected to live at home for longer than seven months. The rest said they planned to move out quickly, but even they might be home longer than expected. According to SmartMoney magazine, the probability of your student getting a job offer upon graduating is about 40% and the average time it takes to find a job is about eight months.[xxvi]

In addition, the stigma of living at home with parents is no longer associated with failure or a lack of achievement. Young adults living with their parents now think of themselves as victims of unfortunate circumstances.[xxvii] In fact, a Pew Research poll indicates that as of 2010, the number of young adults ages 25 to 34 living with their parents increased to 5.9 million.[xxviii]

So your graduate's return to the "empty" nest is a very real possibility. The good news is it doesn't have to be a painful experience for you or your new graduate. If you plan properly, have open and frank conversations, and set reasonable expectations, the results will be a successful launch of your graduate into the real world.

First, you must decide beforehand whether it's okay for your student to come back home and what the ground rules will be. That may sound harsh at first, but every parent and every student is different. Are you doing your graduate a favor or a disservice by allowing him or her to return home? Has your situation changed significantly since they moved out that it could cause serious issues with your marriage or your relationship with your graduate? One of the biggest adjustments that parents have to make is to recognize that their "baby" is now actually a young adult; and they need to be treated that way. Your 18-year old just spent the last four years or more living on their own, making their own decisions, and being free of those old parental rules and responsibilities.

Your student has had a chance to grow up and become an adult. You should expect some tension if you expect the same level of control as you had before they left the house. You are still in control since it is your house, but will you treat your new graduate as your kid, as a guest, as a renter, or something in between?

Map out a Plan

For starters, you'll want a clear sense of the extent of your child's financial problems and the root causes of why they will need to return home. Is this a temporary situation until they begin graduate school in the fall? Are they getting married in six months and just need to stay with you until the wedding? If so, these are normal life patterns and are of little concern since there are already clear exit strategies, so-to-speak. If they are moving home more because they have little choice, then that means having several career and money conversations with your graduate. Do they have a job and can't make ends meet or do they still need to find a job? How much debt do they have and what will be the payments? What will it take financially for them to be able to move out? Once you have a clearer idea of their financial situation, you can begin to set some goals towards helping them move out on their own.

The key to all of this is to put all your and their expectations in writing. How long will they be allowed to stay? What will you and what will you not provide? What will be their financial contribution? What are the rules regarding overnight visitors, chores, and more? By putting everything in writing up front, everyone knows the rules and expectations. It may seem strange to treat your graduate like a business partner or a tenant, but it is a way to guarantee a conversation. Never assume that you and your graduate are on the same page when it comes to why they are returning home, and what their intentions are when it comes to employment, moving out, and even contributing to the household.

Your intent is to derail any "gravy train" before it leaves the station. Yes, you want to help but you don't want the situation to be so comfortable for your graduate such that they have no reason to move out. You don't want to make their return needlessly unpleasant, but you don't want to provide free maid service either. The purpose of allowing them to move back home is to help them get back out again as quickly and on as sound a financial footing as possible.

Give Them an Incentive

Begin by helping your graduate become more responsible. They are adults and should be treated as such. That means they should pay their fair share. They can do this by paying rent or doing household chores, such as laundry or cooking dinners. Nothing will build up resentment faster than you working all day and coming home to a dirty house, no dinner, and your new graduate still in his or her pajamas playing video games or watching television.

For most parents, whether they are willing to admit it or not, having their child move back in with them does cause some stress and interruption in their lives, especially if they are empty nesters. After all, your recent graduate just spent the last four years or more away from home, so you have had time to adjust to life on your own.

Yet, most parents make their new graduate's return somewhat luxurious. Nearly 70% of children living with mom and dad say they are satisfied with their family lives and 44% declare themselves satisfied with their present housing situation.[xxix] As Time Magazine put it, "many young adults don't seem to be in much of a hurry to leave their parents' warm, comfortable nests."[xxx]

Consider charging your new graduate rent. If you are uncomfortable "charging" rent, put the money into a "moving out" account. If they can't pay it now, how will they ever be able to pay it when they move out? Remember, this is about helping them learn financial responsibility, which they need if they ever expect to make it on their own. In this case, you are giving your graduate a chance to understand the responsibilities of living on his or her own within a safe environment. If he or she misses a payment or messes up, you could implement a small financial penalty, but most importantly, you can use that opportunity to discuss with your graduate the serious consequences of making such a mistake in the "real world."

In addition, set an end date. You can set an original move-out date upon graduation, with certain goals that involve their efforts in a job search. As you approach the deadline, you can re-establish a new deadline, but perhaps with greater incentives, such as additional chores. As soon as your graduate finds a job, even if it is not their career job, it is time to review their new financial situation and set a clear goal of their new move-out date. This can always be changed later, but everyone is moving toward the same goal. By setting a move-out date you avoid having the situation drag on. The longer your new graduate stays in the house with you, the more difficult it will become to make the transition to them living on their own. You can always create an automatic increase in monthly "rent" payments after a certain time period. This will allow your graduate to ease out of your house as the payments start to get uncomfortable or approach what they would be paying on their own anyway. And keep in mind, you could be setting this money aside for your graduate to help pay off student loans, purchase new items in their new apartment, and so on.

The Right Balance of Assistance

You can even help with the transition. Surveys indicate that over a quarter of parents help their college graduates with rent and food and more than 10% find themselves helping with college loans or car payments.[xxxi] While this may not be the total independence you and your new graduate were hoping to have, it is a good way to encourage them out of the house. You can slowly wean them from your wallet.

Keep in mind that expectations need to be set with this arrangement too. Otherwise you find yourself resenting the new television or vacation purchase your graduate makes while you are sacrificing your income and your financial goals to assist. The flip side is also true. Your graduate may feel guilty about spending any money on himself or herself because he or she knows you are providing assistance. The key is to make your expectations clear to each other if you are going to assist with monthly bills.

No matter how you handle it, a key element in your relationship with your new graduate is communication. The more clearly you and your graduate can be about communicating expectations and contributions, the easier it will be to avoid a "failure to launch."

A Personal Finance Course for Every Student!

Bring practical, real-world information to your college that your students can use now! Designed by the authors of this book, this course is designed to be taught by almost any department and is open to all students in every major. This course is designed to help students make the most of their money through studying the following strategies:

- Know how those who are helping you are being compensated
- Understand the impact of borrowing money
- Learn the hidden dangers (and benefits) of credit cards
- Negotiate the best price on a car and other major purchases
- Find the best deal on an apartment or house
- Manage the cash that you have
- Learn about hidden rip-offs
- Use your college education to get your dream job
- Invest your money wisely
- Learn how to become a millionaire
- And much more!

More than Just a Textbook

The authors are so passionate about bringing this message to students, not only did they write a textbook, but they also provide one-on-one assistance with any instructor, administrator, or department to help them implement the course from acceptance through promotion.

The instructors have grown their course from 60 students to 500 students per semester on one campus! This is an elective course that students choose to take because they see the value.

If you want to provide a class to your stduents to teach them the basics of personal finance, and want a class of 25 or a class of 500 the authors will help you get there

What Students are Saying about the Course:

"I think that this is one of the most important classes that we will take. I would suggest this class to any of my friends."

"This is probably the best class I have taken in my life. In this class I was able to learn many aspects of finance that I was never taught before. Instructors are funny and enjoyable, great class all around."

"This was an awesome class, never a dull day and it all was useful"

"This course was the most useful class I have taken. Thanks to the instructors!!!"

"The chapters when we learned about interviewing skills, and thank you emails [were most helpful]. It helped me get an internship."

For more information visit: *www.ViaticusGroup.com/books.html*
Or email info@viaticusgroup.com

Need More Copies for Friends?
Want Customized Books for Your Orientation?

How to Keep Your Kid from Moving Back Home after College
is available at quantity discounts for bulk purchases.
Visit *www.ViaticusGroup.com/books.html* for information.

Also available from The Viaticus Group

The Graduate's Guide to Life and Money
Finally, a book designed for recent college graduates that helps them deal with their unique circumstances and challenges with life and money. It includes everything from getting a job, finding an apartment, getting out of debt to getting married! This is a must-have book for the soon-to-be graduate or for anyone under thirty.

Extra Credit: The 7 Things Every College Student
Needs to Know about Credit, Debt & Ca$h
The book every college student needs & every parent wants them to have. More than 1,000 students drop out of college every day due to financial pressure and students graduate with thousands of dollar of student loan *and* credit card debt. It's time to level the playing field by arming students with the information needed to succeed with credit cards, debit cards and student loans.

Visit *www.ViaticusGroup.com/books.html* for ordering information.
Quantity discounts are available for bulk purchases.

The authors are available to speak at your school,
company, organization, or association event.

The Viaticus Group
4104 Sterling Trace Drive
Winterville, NC 28590
301-788-2711
info@viaticusgroup.com
www.ViaticusGroup.com

Bill Pratt

Bill Pratt is the author of several other books on personal finance including *The Graduate's Guide to Life and Money* and *Extra Credit: The 7 Things Every College Student Needs to Know about Credit, Debt & Ca$h*. He also co-authored a textbook. His books help students and young adults improve their finances and their lives.

Bill is a former economist for the federal government and a former vice president for Citigroup. He left the financial industry to focus his efforts on helping others understand money.

Bill is Vice President of The Viaticus Group, a financial education company. He speaks professionally, focusing primarily on colleges. He is also a college instructor at East Carolina University in Greenville, North Carolina. He holds an MBA in finance.

Bill's goal is to help students wade through the endless financial and life decisions they will encounter. By making the best decisions about life and money with the right attitude, Bill believes that people will accumulate more wealth faster and will then be able to use that wealth to improve the lives of those around them.

Mark C. Weitzel

Mark C. Weitzel is the Director of the Financial Wellness Initiative at ECU's College of Business. He is a graduate of the University of Michigan. He earned his Masters in Business Administration from Loyola University of Chicago. He spent 13 years in banking in Detroit, Chicago, and Charlotte. He began as a teller, worked in collections for two years, and rose to Vice President of Branch Operations. He spent several years as regional President and Instructor for the Institute of Financial Education.

Mark is also the Chief Financial Officer of The Viaticus Group, a financial education company. In addition to this book, he also co-authored a personal finance textbook.

In 1993 Mark became a "Mr. Mom" as he walked away from his banking career to raise his three daughters (ages 1, 3 and 4) for the next four years. He began teaching in the Finance Department at ECU in 1998. In 2001 he created ECU's most popular class; Finance 1904, a personal financial management class.

Len Rhodes

Len Rhodes is the Director of Institutional Research at ECU. He is also a graduate of East Carolina University where he earned his Bachelor of Science in Business Administrations with a concentration in accounting and Master in Business Administration degrees. He spent 14 years in small business and entrepreneurship in eastern North Carolina. In 2000 he joined East Carolina University in the management information systems department and later moved to the finance department.

Len is also the President of The Viaticus Group, a financial education company. In addition to this book, he also co-authored a personal finance textbook.

Len's passion is to help students acquire the personal financial decision making skills that help them obtain their personal, professional, and financial goals. Since joining ECU he has accepted positions of greater responsibility, but remains committed to the personal finance class and to the students.

Notes and References

[i] College Board. What It Costs to go to College.
http://www.collegeboard.com/student/pay/add-it-up/4494.html.
Accessed 10/11/2011.

[ii] National Center for Education Statistics. "Recent high school
completers and their enrollment in college, by sex: 1960 through
2009." http://nces.ed.gov/programs/digest/d10/tables/dt10_208.asp.
Accessed 2/11/2012.

[iii] National Center for Education Statistics. "Graduation rates of first-
time postsecondary students who started as full-time degree-seeking
students, by sex, race/ethnicity, time between starting and
graduating, and level and control of institution where student started:
Selected cohort entry years, 1996 through 2004."
http://nces.ed.gov/programs/digest/d09/tables/dt09_331.asp.
Accessed 10/10/2011.

[iv] National Center for Education Statistics. Fast Facts.
http://nces.ed.gov/FastFacts/display.asp?id=76. Accessed 5/8/2012.

[v] Wang, Penelope. "Four myths about college costs: The true price of
that B.A. may not be as high as you think." Money Magazine. January
20, 2005.
http://money.cnn.com/2005/01/20/pf/college/myths_0502/index.ht
m. Accessed 10/11/2011.

[vi] 2009 Honda Civic Ownership Costs. Automobile Magazine. Accessed
5/10/2010.
http://www.automobilemag.com/am/2009/honda/civic/ownership_c
osts.html.

[vii] CarInsurance.com.
http://www.carinsurance.com/kb/content20009.aspx. Accessed
4/7/2012.

[viii] A Total Loss? http://www.edmunds.com/auto-insurance/a-total-loss.html. Accessed 9/3/2011.

[ix] U.S. Department of Education, Federal Student Aid, Student Aid Awareness and Applicant Services. "Funding Education Beyond High School: The Guide to Federal Student Aid 2010-2011." Washington, D.C. 2010.

[x] FinAid. "IRS Dependency Tests." http://www.finaid.org/educators/irsdependent.phtml. Accessed 10/11/2011.

[xi] FinAid. "Dependency Overrides." http://www.finaid.org/educators/pj/dependencyoverrides.phtml. Accessed 10/11/2011.

[xii] Internal Revenue Service. "Tax Benefits for Education." IRS.gov. http://www.irs.gov/newsroom/article/0,,id=213044,00.html. Accessed 12/28/2110.

[xiii] Tompor, Susan. "Student loan debt exceeds credit card debt in USA." USAToday, Detroit Free Press. http://www.usatoday.com/money/perfi/college/2010-09-10-student-loan-debt_N.htm. Accessed 9/10/2010.

[xiv] Lederman, Doug. "The Impact of Student Employment." Inside Higher Ed. June 8, 2009. http://www.insidehighered.com/news/2009/06/08/work. Accessed 3/23/2012.

[xv] Sallie Mae. "Study finds rising number of college students using credit cards for Tuition." Apr 13, 2009. https://www.salliemae.com/about/news_info/newsreleases/041309.htm. Accessed 9/27/2010.

[xvi] U.S. Government. "Fact Sheet: Reforms to Protect American Credit Card Holders." May 22, 2009. http://www.whitehouse.gov/the_press_office/Fact-

Sheet-Reforms-to-Protect-American-Credit-Card-Holders/. Accessed 09/27/2010.

[xvii] Federal Reserve. "New Credit Card Rules Effective Feb 22." http://www.federalreserve.gov/consumerinfo/wyntk_creditcardrules.htm. Accessed 03/30/2011.

[xviii] To calculate the true rate when using a transfer fee, divide one year by the number of months the teaser rate lasts, then multiply that number times the transfer fee. For example, A 6-month teaser rate with a 4% transfer fee is calculated as follows: 12 months / 6 months = 2. Multiply 2 X 4% = 8%. Since a 4% interest rate would have been $40 in interest, they are simply calling it a fee instead, but has the same effect in terms of dollars it costs the consumer. The 8% calculated is considered an effective annual rate since rates are generally annualized to allow for easier comparison.

[xix] CardWeb.com, Inc. ® is a leading publisher of information pertaining to the payment industry, including, but not limited to, credit cards, debit cards, smart cards, prepaid cards, ATM cards, loyalty cards and phone cards. CardWeb.com. http://www.cardweb.com. Accessed 09/27/2010.

[xx] Credit.com. "What is a Schumer Box?" Credit.com. http://www.credit.com/products/credit_cards/schumer-box.jsp. Accessed 09/27/2010.

[xxi] National Association of Attorney's General. www.naag.org. Accessed 11/13/2010.

[xxii] U.S. Department of Education. Sources: http://www2.ed.gov/offices/OSFAP/DirectLoan/RepayCalc/dlentry1.html. http://www.finaid.org/calculators/ibr.phtml. Accessed 04/25/2011.

[xxiii] The Income-Based Repayment has many variables. You will have to use the online calculator and enter your information for a more accurate estimate. For this example the following variables were used, based on the default settings of the finaid.org income-based

repayment calculator: Table Year = 2009, Family Size = 1, Discount Rate = 5.8%, CPI = 3%, State of Residence = Continental U.S., Income Growth Rate = 4%, Poverty Level Change Rate = 3%. In addition the following variables were used for this example: Loan Forgiveness = 25 years, Adjusted Gross Income = $30,000, First Loan = $35,000, Interest Rate = 6.8%, Minimum Payment = $10.00, Interest Rate Reduction = 0%. In this example payments begin at $172 per month and increase each year until year 19 where the payment reaches $403 per month and remains constant for the remaining three years (except the final payment which is $313).

[xxiv] Block, Sandra. "Few options available to help pay off private student loans." USA Today. http://www.usatoday.com/money/perfi/college/story/2012-01-12/private-student-loans-relief/52520848/1. Accessed 1/13/2012.

[xxv] Block. "Few options available to help pay off private student loans."

[xxvi] Kadet, Anne. "Job Hunting: A Family Affair ." SmartMoney March 2012: 64-71.

[xxvii] Tuttle, Brad. "Being 30 and Living With Your Parents Isn't Lame - It's Awesome." Time. Moneyland. March 20, 2012. http://moneyland.time.com/2012/03/20/being-30-and-living-with-your-parents-isnt-lame-its-awesome/#ixzz1pkkSXovO. Accessed 3/21/2012.

[xxviii] Tuttle, Brad. "More Young Adults are Poor, Living with Their Parents." Time. Moneyland. September 14, 2011. http://moneyland.time.com/2011/09/14/more-young-adults-are-poor-live-with-their-parents/. Accessed 3/21/2012.

[xxix] Parker, Kim. "The Boomerang Generation: Feeling OK about Living with Mom and Dad." Pew Research Center. March 15, 2012. http://www.pewsocialtrends.org/2012/03/15/the-boomerang-generation/1/. Accessed 3/21/2012.

[xxx] Tuttle, Brad. "Being 30 and Living With Your Parents Isn't Lame - It's Awesome."

[xxxi] Kadet, Anne. 64-71.

NOTES:

NOTES:

NOTES:

NOTES:

NOTES:

Made in the USA
Lexington, KY
10 March 2015